William James's Philosophy

Marcus
Peter
Ford

William James's Philosophy
A New Perspective

The University of Massachusetts Press Amherst

Copyright © 1982 by
The University of Massachusetts Press
All rights reserved
Printed in the United States of America
Library of Congress Cataloging in Publication Data
Ford, Marcus Peter, 1950–
William James's philosophy.
Includes bibliographical references and index.
1. James, William, 1842–1910.   1. Title.
B945.J24F67   191   81–16314
ISBN 0–87023–366–1   AACR2

This book is dedicated to my wife
Sandra Lubarsky

Contents

Preface

I have spent several years trying to understand William James's philosophy. These years have been most enjoyable. I have enjoyed learning from and wrestling with James and I have enjoyed working with other scholars who are also interested in James's thought. David R. Griffin, Professor of Philosophy of Religion at the School of Theology at Claremont, has been especially influential in my thinking on James. Many of "my ideas" were first "his ideas." John K. Roth, Professor of Philosophy at Claremont Men's College, has also aided my understanding of James. Together they have helped me to think more clearly and to write more precisely. John McDermott, Professor of Philosophy at Texas A&M, also played a role in my thinking. He read an earlier draft of this book and offered many valuable suggestions. McDermott understands James differently than I do, but he took the time to improve my work in order that my position might be clearly presented.

I have also enjoyed the total support of my parents, my wife, and my friend, Gary Bollinger, while writing this book. They have sustained me. My wife, Sandra Lubarsky, in addition to lending support, has been involved in the writing of this book. She has offered many suggestions for improving the clarity of the text and has helped me understand some of the details of James's arguments that I had overlooked.

Mary Tookey also read the manuscript and greatly improved the grammar and, in some instances, the style. Mary teaches English at Eureka College where I teach philosophy. Eureka College, located in Eureka, Illinois, is committed to scholarly work and has provided funds that have been used to write this book.

Parts of chapters 4 and 5 have been published in the *Proceedings of the Charles S. Peirce Society* and part of chapter 3 has appeared in the *Southern Journal of Philosophy*. I wish to thank both of these scholarly journals for their permission to include this material. I would also like to express my gratitude to Harvard University Press for their definitive editions of James's works. *The Works of William James,* under the general editorship of Frederick H. Burkhardt, has provided the James scholar with a standard edition of James's texts.

Finally, I would like to acknowledge Leone Stein, the Director of the University of Massachusetts Press, and her staff, Hanna Hopp, Pamela Campbell, and Ralph Kaplan. I have encountered none of the awful experiences that one often associates with the publication of a book. I feel fortunate for the opportunity to have worked with them.

I take full responsibility for what I have written, but I cannot take all the credit. I am indebted to all of the people mentioned above and to others whose influence and support have been more indirect. These individuals have made this book possible and have made the actual writing of it very pleasant.

It is an exaggeration to attribute a general change in a climate of thought to any one piece of writing, or to any one author. No doubt Descartes only expressed definitely and in a decisive form what was already in the air of his period. Analogously, in attributing to William James the inauguration of a new stage in philosophy, we should be neglecting other influences of his time. But, admitting this, there still remains a certain fitness in contrasting his essay, "Does Consciousness Exist," published in 1904, with Descartes' Discourse on Method, *published in 1637. James clears the stage of the old paraphernalia; or rather he entirely alters its lighting.*

ALFRED NORTH WHITEHEAD
Science and the Modern World, 1925

Introduction

More books have been written on William James than on any other American philosopher. One can only speculate why this is so. Perhaps it is because James addresses himself to major issues and writes with much charm and insight. Perhaps his work is not clear and cries out for clarification. Perhaps it is because James is largely correct in his beliefs but that they need updating. Or, more cynically, perhaps writers seek to legitimize their own views by falsely ascribing them to a respected figure of the past. In my estimation all these factors have played a role in the amount of attention James's works have received. My reasons for writing this book are to explicate James's thought on important issues, to point to what I consider to be his most valuable insights, and to suggest how he might have been more consistent in his philosophy. In large measure my interest is historical; I feel that it is important to determine just exactly what James thought. In addition to my historical concern, however, I believe that many of his insights are almost entirely correct—that is, that quite often his position corresponds with the way things actually are. I have tried not to confuse my historical interest with my personal beliefs. For the most part I regard my agreement with James as coincidental.

I think that the majority of James's interpreters have misconstrued his thought, or, at least, that major elements of his thought have been ignored or poorly understood. In specific I think that his pragmatic theory of truth and his metaphysical position are widely misinterpreted. James's pragmatic theory of truth is basically realistic, i.e., a correspondence theory;

and his metaphysical position is a panpsychic type of metaphysical realism. Ralph Ross, Charles Morris, A. J. Ayer, and H. S. Thayer, to name but a few, have misunderstood James's pragmatic theory of truth in various ways. Ralph Barton Perry, Ralph Ross, Edward Madden, and Peter Hare are among those who have misunderstood James's metaphysical position. Naturally one needs to be cautious when challenging the conclusions of capable scholars, but one cannot simply accept the judgments of others, especially when their judgments are mutually incompatible. I have sought to correct past mistakes and to offer new interpretations where old ones seem to be inadequate or simply wrong.

Several factors are responsible for the traditional misunderstanding of James's pragmatic theory of truth. In part it is caused by misunderstandings concerning James's metaphysical position and in part it is caused by James's own confusions. It is also partly because some have been too eager to see James as a contemporary of the mid- and late-twentieth century. James's book, *The Meaning of Truth,* is a collection of articles written over a period of twenty-four years and some rather heated responses to various interpretations of his theory of truth. James tries to harmonize his earlier views with his later views by adding footnotes to his early articles and he tries to clarify his position in light of what he considered to be inexcusable misinterpretations of this theory. Nonetheless, no single meaning of "truth" emerges from the book. He objects to the Absolutists' theory of truth and claims to be within the realist tradition, and yet he identifies his position with F. C. S. Schiller's and John Dewey's. Ralph Ross, Charles Morris, and A. J. Ayer believe that James's pragmatic theory of truth is itself nonrealistic or unrealistic. Edward C. Moore, H. S. Thayer, and John E. Smith are among the very few who contend that James's pragmatic theory of truth is finally realistic—which is to say that it is a variety of the traditional correspondence theory of truth. I argue that Moore, Thayer, and Smith are correct in their judgment, though I disagree with certain aspects of Thayer's understanding of James's theory of truth. James is a metaphysical realist (of the panpsychic variety) and his pragmatic theory of truth, with all its confusions, presupposes a correspondence between ideas and objects that exist independently of anyone else's experience of them.

James's metaphysical position, his panpsychic version of metaphysical realism, is even less commonly understood than his pragmatic theory of truth. Bruce Kuklick is virtually alone in his recognition that James is finally a panpsychist.[1] Perry, and more recently, Madden and Hare, recognize that James is a realist and they acknowledge that for a certain period of time James is attracted to panpsychism; but they fail to understand the extent of James's commitment to panpsychism.[2] In all fairness to those that have not understood James's metaphysical position, it should be stated that he is not primarily concerned with developing a metaphysical position and that, when he is not explicitly concerned with metaphysical issues, he usually adopts the prevailing metaphysical assumption of his time. To complicate matters even further, he writes a series of articles which were eventually published under the title of *Essays in Radical Empiricism,* in which he suggests the possibility that the ultimate units of reality are "pure experiences" that are neither mental nor physical but potentially either or both. This position, which is commonly referred to as his "radical empiricism," is not the only metaphysical position expressed in *Essays in Radical Empiricism;* but, for various reasons, this "neutral monism," as it has also been termed, is usually regarded as James's final metaphysical stance. It is not.

Recently some have argued that James is a proto-phenomenologist or that he has no metaphysical position at all. Bruce Wilshire, James Edie, and John Wild are prominent among those who see James as some kind of phenomenologist, although they are not in perfect agreement as to what kind of phenomenologist he is. Edie and Wild, however, agree with Wilshire's contention that "far too much emphasis has heretofore been placed on his later pragmatic theory of truth and on his occasional pieces of philosophy of life and oracular metaphysics, and not enough stress upon his earlier theory of meaning, as found in the *Principles,* together with the sketch of a systematic metaphysics that emerges directly from it."[3] According to Wilshire, Edie, and Wild, the "sketch of a metaphysics" that emerges directly from *The Principles of Psychology* is a type of phenomenology. They are to be thanked for bringing James's psychology text back into public attention and for their illumination of some of its contents, but I cannot concur with their judgment that James is best understood *überhaupt* as some type of phenomenologist.

Other interpreters take the position that James is not interested in doing traditional metaphysics at all. Henry Levinson, for example, comments, "If ontological statements amount to statements that make categorical claims about what there is, then James does not make any [ontological statements]."[4] According to Levinson, James is a psychologist, a moral philosopher, and a religious thinker, but not a metaphysician. Patrick Dooley agrees. In his book, *Pragmatism as Humanism,* Dooley brings these aspects of James's thought together under the concept of "humanism." Levinson and Dooley and those who share their contention that James does not do metaphysics in the traditional sense of ontology are simply mistaken. James is interested in psychology, moral philosophy, and religious questions, but he is also interested in constructing a metaphysics in the traditional meaning of the term. In the epilogue of *Psychology: The Briefer Course,* James gives the classical definition of "metaphysics" as the arbitrator of "all the special sciences." "The special sciences all deal with data that are full of obscurity and contradiction; but from the point of view of their limited purposes these defects may be overlooked. . . . But it is obvious that problems irrelevant from one standpoint may be essential from another. And as soon as one's purpose is the attainment of the maximum of possible insight into the world as a whole, the metaphysical puzzles become the most urgent of all."[5] Metaphysics, for James, is the first science, the ground from which each of the special sciences—ethics, physics, psychology—are "subject to revision in the light of each other's needs."[6] There is no good reason to suppose that James had another definition of "metaphysics" in mind when he wrote to Henri Bergson in 1902. "My health is so poor now that work goes on very slowly, but I am going, if I live, to write a general system of metaphysics which in many fundamental ideas agrees closely with what you have set forth, and the agreement inspires and encourages me more than you well imagine."[7] When James says in 1902 that he intends to write a "general system of metaphysics" similar to Bergson's, he is not, I submit, referring to a metaphysics without ontology as Levinson suggests nor is he referring to a humanism as Dooley maintains. By "metaphysics" he means first philosophy, the science of what things are.

The metaphysical position that James endorses may be termed "panpsychism" or, more generally, "pansubjectivism." It is a variety of metaphysical or ontological realism in that it holds that there exists in some mode of actuality a plurality of individual entities that are not dependent upon anyone (at least anyone *else's*) awareness of them. For the panpsychist there is nothing apart from all experience, because things are self-experiencing, but things can and do exist independently of anyone *else's* experience of them. In 1903 James associates his term "radical empiricism" with panpsychism.

> If empiricism is to be radical it must indeed admit the concrete data of experience in their full completeness. The only fully complete data are, however, the successive moments of our own several histories, taken with their "objective" deliverance or "content." After the analogy of these moments of experiences must all complete reality be conceived. Radical empiricism thus leads to the assumption of a collectivism of personal lives (which may be of any grade of complication, and superhuman or infrahuman as well as human), variously cognitive of each other, variously conative and impulsive, genuinely evolving and changing by effort and trial, and by their interaction and cumulative achievements making up the world.[8]

And in 1908, in his "Miller-Bode" notebooks, he writes ". . . the constitution of reality that I am making for is of [the] psychic type."[9]

In chapter 1, I discuss what I take to be the most important aspects of James's great work, *The Principles of Psychology.* It has been said that all James's later works are latent within the two volumes that comprise *The Principles of Psychology.* This is, of course, an overstatement but it is based on a fact: the positions that James enunciates in *The Principles of Psychology,* especially his process view of the self, are very important to James's subsequent thought. In chapter 1, I discuss James's view of the self, his critique of other psychologies, his understanding of experience, and his concern about his process understanding of the self.

In chapter 2, I deal with James's thought concerning religion and science. More specifically I deal with the essays that make up *The Will to Believe and Other Essays in Popular Philosophy.* It is widely assumed that science and religion are incompatible: that science rules out the possibility of a divine reality and, in doing so, rules out the possibility of a moral standard in the universe. In *The Will to Believe* James argues against this assumption. One can be religious, and one can be an ethical absolutist, without being unscientific. Religion and science are not mutually exclusive.

Chapter 3 is devoted to James's understanding of God and to his commitment to ontological or metaphysical pluralism. James is famous for the war he waged against Absolute Idealism, and yet, when carefully considered, James's pluralism is not as pluralistic as it is usually taken to be. In *The Varieties of Religious Experience, A Pluralistic Universe,* and elsewhere, James holds the position that everything—at least every conscious self—is literally *in* God. James's "pluralism" is almost always a qualified pluralism and not a radical pluralism.

My fourth chapter is given to James's pragmatic theory of truth. In my estimation, James's theory of truth as expressed in *The Meaning of Truth* stands as his most confused effort. I have tried to unsnarl his statements and to make his theory of truth conform to his fundamental belief in a world that exists independently of anyone's perception of it—or more precisely, his belief in objects that exist independently of someone or something else's experience of them.

In chapter 5, I trace the development of James's metaphysical speculations. His panpsychism is never systematically developed nor is it very sophisticated. Nonetheless, he is a panpsychist.

The purpose of chapter 6 is to show how James's most significant insights and his most fundamental concepts lend themselves to systemization. In this chapter I draw heavily from Alfred North Whitehead's philosophy. Whitehead, like James, is a panpsychist realist (or more correctly, a pansubjectivist realist) and, like James, views the self as a society of momentary events. There are other important similarities: both affirm real pluralism and real togetherness in the world; both hold that relations are directly experienced; both view reality to be "in the making"—to be quantitatively increasing; and both see God as active in the natural world and as being limited by other actualities. Other similarities exist, but these are the most striking and the most significant. In that chapter, I examine the areas of agreement between James's and Whitehead's thought and use Whitehead's metaphysical system to suggest how James might have brought his doctrines and insights together into a unified philosophical position.

There are those who will strenuously object to my using Whitehead to understand James and who will point to James's statements against systematic philosophy and to his remarks that philosophies are simply psychological projections as irrefutable evidence that James and Whitehead are worlds apart in their philosophies. According to James, "*Technical* writing on *philosophical* subjects . . . is certainly a crime against the human race!"[10] and

Pretend what we may, the whole man within us is at work when we form our philosophical opinions. Intellect, will, tastes, and passions co-operate just as they do in practical affairs; and lucky it is if the passion be not something as petty as a love of personal conquest over the philosopher across the way. . . . It is almost incredible that men who are themselves working philosophers should pretend that any philosophy can be, or ever has been, constructed without the help of personal preference, belief, or divination.[11]

These two sentiments are characteristically Jamesian but they are not wholly representative. The same James who curses technical philosophy curses his own "popular style." Writing to F. C. S. Schiller about his decision to give the Hibbert Lectures, which were later published under the title of *A Pluralistic Universe,* James writes, "This job condemns me to publish another book written in picturesque and popular style when I was settling down to something whose manner would be more *strengwissenschaftlich,* i.e., concise, dry, and impersonal."[12] And the James who speaks of one's character determining one's philosophy is the same person who argues so ardently for real freedom and who speaks about actualities that exist independently of human opinions and partially determine what can and cannot be thought about them. "Grant . . . that our human subjectivity determines *what* we shall say things are," James says, "grant that it gives the 'predicates' to all the 'subjects' of our conversation. Still the fact remains that some subjects are there for us to talk about, and others are not there; and that farther fact that, in spite of so many different ways in which we may perform the talking, there still is a grain in the subjects which we can't well go against, a cleavage-structure which resists certain of our predicates and makes others slide in more easily."[13]

James is leery of technical philosophy because he knows that one can use it to deny obvious truths and he is suspicious of philosophers who claim complete objectivity for their thought. However, his suspicions run only so deep. He realizes the advantages of technical philosophy as well as its dangers, and he knows the absurdity of radical subjectivism or solipsism as well as the absurdity of complete objectivity. Speaking from a psychological perspective, one's character is largely determinative of how one views reality, but from a philosophical perspective—at least from the philosophical perspective of a metaphysical realist—there is a world that exists independently of all human temperaments and projections. Past and present facts are just what they are regardless of what anyone (any human) believes or needs to believe. James knows this full well even though he is not always clear in his own mind how to reconcile this with his belief in the open universe and the ability of an individual to affect the outcome of the world.

Temperamentally, James is ill-suited to construct a well-rounded system in which everything has a place. He is too eager to get into the thick of things. He is too impatient and too colorful in his language, and yet he recognizes the importance of systematic thought. Near the end of his life he was at work on a manuscript he entitled *Some Problems of Philosophy: A Beginning of an Introduction to Philosophy.* In the instruction he left with the manuscript he writes: "Say that I hoped by it to round out my system, which now is too much like an arch built on one side."[14] He never constructed the other side of the arch and it is not likely that he would have had he lived several years longer; system-building was not his forte. One can, however, picture the other half of the arch— one can see what is necessary to keep the half of an arch he built from falling. Whitehead's "philosophy of organism" is the other half of James's arch. In the preface to *Process and Reality* Whitehead states that one of his "preoccupations" has been to rescue William James's philosophy "from the charge of anti-intellectualism, which rightly or wrongly has been associated with it." In my estimation he is successful.

1 Important Aspects of James's Psychology

In 1890 James published his great two-volume work, *The Principles of Psychology*. He was forty-eight years old when it was published and had been working on it for over twelve years. Much of what it contains was not new; the work is full of reports and summaries of the discoveries and theories of other psychologists. But what is new is significant—both positively and negatively so—for James's subsequent thought. And some of what is not new takes on a new meaning in light of James's new insights. In this chapter I will focus on the important aspects of James's psychology.

The most significant feature of James's psychology is his process view of the self—the "stream of thought." Other important features of his psychology are his analysis of an experience or thought and his denial of unconscious experience. According to James, thoughts are wholly private; they include the experience of relations; they are "fringed"; and they are teleological in nature—they are what he calls "fighters for ends." James's assessment of psychology in general and his dissatisfaction with some of his own theories are also important.

James's process psychology stands in opposition to several types of substance psychologies, most notably the "mind-stuff theory," the "associationist theory" and the "spiritualists" or "transcendentalist theory."[1] Despite obvious differences, each of these theories shares a common presupposition: that there are psychic substances. For each of these psychologies the self or the phenomenal self is a substance or is made up of substances. The "mind-stuffists" contend that each complex moment of human experience is actually a compound of conscious units or substances; the associationists maintain that complex experience is a compound of simple, substancelike, sensations; and the spiritualists or transcendentalists maintain that the self is actually an enduring mental substance. In each case the final psychological actuality is considered to be a substance or a collection of substances. James rejects these substance psychologies in favor of a process view of experience and of the self. According to his process psychology, new experiences are actually new experiences and not merely the regrouping of units of consciousness or sensations, and the self is not an enduring substance but rather a series of new experiences. Before examining James's process psychology, it is helpful to take a closer look at the various substance psychologies he rejects and his reasons for doing so.

"The theory of 'mind-stuff,' " James writes, "is the theory that our [human] mental states are compounds. . . ." The mind-stuffists or "mind dusters" argue that all "new forms" of physical existence are only the redistribution of the original and unchanging atoms of the universe. In their opinion: "The self-same atoms which, chaotically dispersed, made the nebula, now jammed and temporarily caught in peculiar positions, form our brains; and the 'evolution' of the brains, if understood, would be simply the account of how the atoms came to be so caught and jammed. In this story no new *natures*, no factors not present at the beginning, are introduced at any later stage."[2]

The mind-stuffists believe that what is true of biological evolution is also true of experiential or mental evolution. Higher forms of experience, such as human experience, are only a particular combination of preexistent bits of experience: "Just as the material atoms have formed bodies and brains by massing themselves together, so the mental atoms, by an analogous process of aggregation, have fused into those larger consciousnesses which we know in ourselves and suppose to exist in our fellow-animals."[3]

James criticizes the mind-stuff theory on empirical and logical grounds. His empirical objection was that what is given in introspection is a whole experience and not a multitude of component parts fitted together. His logical objection is that atoms of feeling—if they are in fact substancelike units—cannot be said to form meaningful wholes, for to be a substance is to be a self-existent being.[4] James wrote:

Take a hundred of them [elemental units of consciousness], shuffle them and pack them as close together as you can (whatever that may mean): still each remains the same feeling it always was, shut in its own skin, windowless, ignorant of what the other feelings are and mean. There would be a hundred-and-first feeling there, if, when a group or series of such feelings were set up, a consciousness *belonging to the group as such* should emerge. And this 101st feeling would be a totally new fact; the 100 original feelings might, by a curious physical law, be a signal for its *creation* when they came together; but they would have no substantial identity with it, nor it with them, and one could never deduce the one from the others, or (in any intelligible sense) say that they *evolved* it.[5]

A hundred individual feelings do not constitute the *feeling*-of-a-hundred-feelings. The feeling-of-a-hundred-feelings is itself an additional feeling—"a totally new fact." It is something other than the mere multitude of feelings.

The second major substance psychology James rejects is the associationist theory.[6] The associationist theory, advocated by David Hume and John Mill, is similar to the mind-stuff theory in some respects. "The ordinary associationist-psychology supposes . . . that whenever an object of thought contains many elements, the thought itself must be made up of just as many elements, one idea for each element, and all fused together in appearance, but really separate.[7] In his famous chapter, "Personal Identity," in *Treatise on Human Nature*, Hume ventures to affirm that an individual is "*nothing but a bundle or collection of different perceptions,* which succeed each other with inconceivable rapidity, and are in a perpetual flux and movement."[8] Moreover, Hume maintains: "All our distinct perceptions are distinct existences, and the mind never perceives any real connection among distinct existences. Did our perceptions either inhere in something simple or individual, or *did the mind perceive some real connection* among them, there would be no difficulty in the case."[9]

Most scholars have not regarded the associationist theory as a type of substance psychology simply because the associationists deny (at least formally) the existence of the substantial self. This is perfectly legitimate, but it overlooks the fact that what Hume called a "perception" or an "impression" fits the Cartesian definition of a substance, namely, that which requires nothing but itself in order to exist. Hume himself pointed this out. "My conclusion . . . is that since all our perceptions are different from each other, and from every thing else in the universe, they are also distinct and separable, and may be considered as separately existent, and have no need of anything else to support their existence. They are therefore substances, as far as this definition explains a substance."[10] Hume, then, is a substantialist in this sense: although he denied (at least formally) the substantial self, he replaced it with a bundle of perceptions, each of which is itself a substance. In this respect the associationist theory is rightly classified as a substance psychology for it has a substance theory of experience.

James's rejection of Humean associationism was complete. In his estimation the associationists are guilty of three major mistakes: first, supposing that because the object of a thought may be analyzed into simpler parts the thought itself consists of simpler elements; second, denying the feeling of relation that qualifies later feelings in terms of earlier feelings; and third, "smuggling in surreptitiously" the concept of an active agent—a self—after they have denied such an entity. The first mistake is what James later calls "vicious intellectualism"—the habit of analyzing particulars strictly in terms of the universals they embody. The second error is purely empirical. James argues that the feeling of "A preceded by B" is a different feeling from "A preceded by C" and therefore what is not felt is first "B" and then "A," or first "C" and then "A," but first "B" and then "A as preceded by B," or first "C" and then "A as preceded by C." This is what James calls the "feeling of relation" and this is what Hume and the associationists deny. The third error is one of inconsistency. On the one hand the associationists deny the existence of an active self and on the other hand they presuppose it. Note, for example, the passage quoted above: ". . . and *the mind* never perceives any real connection. . . ." According to James: "As a rule, associationist writers keep talking about 'the mind' and about what 'we' do; and so, smuggling in surreptitiously what they ought avowedly to have postulated in the form of a present 'judging Thought.' . . ."[11] On the one hand the associationists maintain that the self is "nothing but a bundle or collection of different perceptions" and on the other hand, they talk about a "mind" or a "self" that does not perceive any connections between individual perceptions. In short, the associationist theory is logically mistaken, empirically inadequate, and finally inconsistent.

The third major type of substance psychology James rejects is the "spiritualist" or the "transcendentalist" psychology.

The spiritualists affirm the substantial self that is denied (at least formally) by the associationists. For the spiritualist or the transcendentalist, the self is actually an immortal soul, that is, a spiritual substance.

The Soul . . . exists as a *simple spiritual substance* [my emphasis] in which the various psychic faculties, operations, and affections inhere.

If we ask what a Substance is, the only answer is that it is a self-existent being, or one which needs no other subject in which to inhere. . . . The *consequences* of the simplicity and the substantiality of the Soul are its incorruptibility and natural immortality—nothing but God's direct *fiat* can annihilate it—and its *responsibility* at all times for whatever it may have ever done.

. . . [T]ranscendentalism is only Substantialism grown shamefaced and the Ego is only a "cheap and nasty" edition of the soul.[12]

Clearly James identifies Kant's theory of the transcendental ego with the classical concept of the substantial soul, and by "substantial" James meant "self-existing being or one which needs no other subject in which to inhere."

According to James, most Western thinkers have endorsed this substantial theory of the self. In addition to Kant he mentions Plato, Aristotle, most of the medievalists, Hobbes, Descartes, Locke, Leibnitz, Wolf, and Berkeley.[13] Each of these individuals, he contends, regards the self as an enduring, self-sufficient entity.

In James's opinion, the substantial theory of the self provides the classical Christian thinkers with a philosophical explanation for the immortality of the human soul and for forensic responsibility before God. This, of course, is not Kant's attraction to the theory. Kant had "practical" reasons for believing in personal immortality and for forensic responsibility before God. Kant's motivation is purely theoretical; he wants to provide a principle of unity upon which to ground Humean perceptions or sensa. His aim is to bring Hume's disjointed perceptions together in the transcendental ego.

James is not subtle in his rejection of the "soul-theory." "The Soul-theory," he contends, "is . . . a complete superfluity, so far as accounting for the actually verified facts of conscious experience." And he calls Kant's transcendental ego, ". . . as ineffectual and windy an abortion as Philosophy can show." In James's eyes, Hume is mistaken in his judgment that perceptions are substancelike units, totally self-sufficient and shut-off from each other, and hence James sees no need to posit an additional substance within which to house these perceptions. Kant provides an artificial solution to an artificial problem. Even if Hume had been correct in his analysis of perceptions, merely locating these perceptions in an additional substance (as if one substance could actually be "in" another substance) would not bring them into unity with each other. "The only service that transcendent egoism has done to psychology," James maintains, "has been by its protest against Hume's 'bundle'-theory of the mind."[14]

When set beside the substance psychologies that dominated Western thought, the revolutionary nature of James's process psychology is all the more evident. Having rejected the possibility that a complex moment of human experience might actually be a compound of individual units and having rejected the notion of the substantial self or "soul," James puts forth his view of experience and of the self. According to James the self is nothing more than a series of experiences, or what he also called "thoughts" or "feelings." Unlike the "spiritualist" or "transcendentalist" theory of the self, which assumes an enduring entity (a substance) in addition to the flux of experience, James's theory of the self presupposes no such entity. The conscious self, he maintains "as a psychological fact, can be fully described without supposing any other agent than a succession of perishing thoughts, endowed with the functions of appropriation and rejection and of which some can know and appropriate or reject objects already known, appropriated or rejected by the rest."[15] For James the self is constituted solely of experience, past and present. There is no transexperiential actuality that unifies experience and *is* the self; experience, past and present, is all there is.

The distinction between past experiences and present experiences is important. James speaks of the self as constituted of two components: first, the "objective person" and second, the passing subjective thought or feeling that knows or owns the objective person. The objective person he terms the "me"; the perishing pulse of subjectivity he terms the "I." "The consciousness of Self involves a stream of thought each part of which as 'I' can (1) remember those [I-s] which went before, and know the things they knew; and (2) emphasize and care paramountly for certain ones among them as *'me'* and *appropriate to these* the rest."[16] The self, then, for James is not a substance or a collection of substancelike things; it is a "stream of thoughts" or, as he sometimes calls it, a "chain of past selves."

Metaphysically, the metaphor matters; a "stream" and a "chain" have different characteristics. Before one examines the differences, however, more needs to be said about the "I," the momentary thought or feeling that appropriates or rejects the "me-s." Most of the other significant features of James's psychology are present in his analysis of a "thought." James discerns five characteristics all thoughts have in common:

1. Every thought tends to be part of a personal consciousness.
2. Within each personal consciousness thought is always changing.
3. Within each personal consciousness thought is sensibly continuous.
4. It [thought] always appears to deal with objects independent of itself.
5. It [thought] is interested in some parts of these objects to the exclusion of others, and welcomes or rejects—*chooses* from among them, in a word, all the while.[17]

First, "Every thought tends to be a part of a personal consciousness." By this James means that there are no thoughts in general. There are my thoughts, your thoughts, and someone else's thoughts, but there are no thoughts that belong to no one in particular. To say that "the United States of America thinks that . . ." or that "the class thinks . . ." is to speak loosely. Thoughts belong to individual selves. Everyone in the United States of America may think such and such and everyone in a class may agree on some issue, but countries and classes do not think. This also means that particular individuals do not "share thoughts." Two individuals may have similar thoughts, but they cannot partake of one and the same thought. Individuals are cut off from the subjective experience of other individuals. "No thought ever comes into direct *sight* of a thought in another personal consciousness than its own. Absolute insulation, irreducible pluralism, is the law. . . . Neither contemporaneity, nor proximity in space, nor similarity of quality and content are able to fuse thoughts, which are sundered by this barrier of belonging to different personal minds. The breaches between such thoughts are the most absolute breaches in nature." James is willing to make some exceptions in the cases of individuals with multiple personalities,[18] but otherwise he is adamant that thoughts are owned by one and only one individual. "Absolute insulation, irreducible pluralism," he contends, "is the law."

This notion of "absolute insulation" or "irreducible pluralism" is very significant in terms of his subsequent philosophy. In *A Pluralistic Universe* he revokes this "law" and permits the overlapping of consciousness. Ironically, repeal of the law of absolute insulation mitigates the "irreducible pluralism" of reality so that James's stated position in *A Pluralistic Universe* is less pluralistic than he intended it to be. At any rate, in *The Principles of Psychology* each thought belongs to one, and only one, self.

Second, "Within each personal consciousness thought is always changing." By this James means that no one can have the same thought twice. Hearing a certain note for the second time is an experience different from hearing it for the first time or hearing it for the third time. The "sameness" of two experiences is an abstraction. Each experience, in its concrete wholeness, is different from all other experiences. Moreover, with each passing moment one's self is increased so that one is not the same self at a later time. "Experience is remoulding us every moment, and our mental reaction on every given thing is really a result of our experience of the whole world up to that date."[19]

Third, "Within personal consciousness thought is sensibly continuous." Each thought feels itself to belong to certain prior thoughts even when it is separated from those prior thoughts by dreamless sleep or a prolonged period of unconsciousness. In order to explain this phenomenon James introduces the feeling of relations, the psychic overtone or "fringe," and what he terms "animal warmth." The experience of relation permits a thought to feel itself *as related to* previous thoughts. That thoughts are constituted partially by their relations to prior thoughts is an important insight on James's part and one that he was later to call radical empiricism's "statement of fact." Relations, as well as objects, are experienced. "There is not a conjunction or a preposition, and hardly an adverbial phrase, syntactic form, or inflection of voice, in human speech, that does not express some shading or other of relations which we at some moment actually feel to exist between the larger objects of our thought.... We ought to say a feeling of *and*, a feeling of *if*, a feeling of *but*, and a feeling of *by*, quite as readily as we say a feeling of *blue* or a feeling of *cold*."[20]

Relations, for the most part, are not *clearly* felt. A thought or a moment of experience has both a center and a fringe. The object or topic of an experience occupies the center while the feelings of relation exist in the "fringe." When one is concerned only with the object or topic of thoughts, experience appears to be discontinuous; nonetheless, the experiences of relations that exist in the fringe of a thought tie thoughts together.

"Animal warmth" denotes the vague quality that distinguishes a thought belonging to one self from the thought of another self. "Each thought, out of a multitude of other thoughts of which it may think, is able to distinguish those which belong to its own Ego from those which do not. The former have a warmth and intimacy about them of which the latter are completely devoid, being merely conceived, in a cold and foreign fashion, and not appearing as blood-relatives, bringing their greetings to us from out of the past."[21] The particular warmth that a thought has serves as a brand. Any thought bearing that brand belongs to the same self. Even when a thought is separated from the previous thoughts of the same self by some period of time, it recognizes its predecessors as *its* predecessors.

In summary, within personal consciousness thought is sensibly continuous because each thought carries a brand—a brand of "animal warmth"—and because relations are felt. Most of the time the feelings of relations are felt only dimly, on the fringe of conscious experience. The mood or the emotional framework within which the objects or topics of thought exist, is these vague feelings of relations. In the case of remembrance, when the distance between a thought and its predecessor is great, the feeling of relation is not vague but central. To remember is to feel a direct relation to some particular past thought or thoughts *as past.* Without the experience of being related to past thoughts *as past,* past thoughts are not experienced *as remembered.*

Fourth, "It [thought] always appears to deal with objects independent of itself." Thoughts appear to be thoughts about something that exists independently of being thought. James realizes the problems associated with epistemological realism and does not want to get involved in these. Whether or not thought in fact deals with objects independent of itself, it does *appear* to. As a psychologist, James is content to leave the matter at that.

Fifth, "It [thought] is always more interested in one part of its object than in another, and welcomes and rejects, or chooses, all the while it thinks." Thought or experience is not strictly passive—it acts. Thought is teleological; it pursues goals of its own, it is a "fighter for ends" and it welcomes, rejects, and chooses experience in light of its ends. The teleological nature of experience, which James attests to in *The Prin-*

ciples of Psychology, plays an important role in his "pragmatic theory of truth." Thought is not simply a reactor to stimuli; it is also an actor. Thought both finds a world and creates one.

James discusses this characteristic of thought in terms of sense experience and in terms of appropriating the past thoughts that are one's self. Sense organs are organs of selection. They abstract only certain aspects of objects, and only certain of these abstractions are attended to by conscious thought. There are more sounds than are heard; and most of the sounds that are, in one sense, "heard" are ignored. And the same is true with the other senses. Only a small part of the information that is received physiologically registers in conscious thought. Ignoring some of what is available to conscious experience emphasizes what is consciously considered. In terms of survival this is often very important. Not everything in one's environment merits undivided attention even if it were possible to give it. By ignoring some things and emphasizing others, thought is free to deal more effectively with those things in the world that are, in one sense or another, more important.

Thought is also active in its appropriation of past thoughts. The present thought has a degree of freedom in how it appropriates its past. It is free to welcome past thoughts or accept them begrudgingly; it is free to emphasize certain past thoughts and to virtually ignore others, depending on the aims of the present thought. In *The Principles of Psychology*, James writes: "There must be an agent of the appropriating and disowning; but the agent we have already named. It is the Thought to whom the various 'constituents' are known. That Thought is the vehicle of choice as well as of cognition; and among the choices it makes are these appropriations, or repudiations, of its 'own.' "[22] The present thought decides, as it were, what to make of its past. The past thoughts or experiences are just what they are; they cannot be changed. But the present thought has some degree of freedom in *how* it takes account of them.

James's realization that thought is active as well as passive does not make him a Kantian. James rejects Kant's theory of the transcendental self and Kant's categories of understanding. His acknowledgment that there is an active component of experience, however, does differentiate James from the British Empiricist school of thought. For James, each thought is partially responsible for itself—it is partially responsible for its experience or thought. The events in the past are settled once and for all and so are the objects in the physical world, but how they are experienced is not already determined. Within limits, each thought is free to determine itself.

One important aspect of James's psychology that is not explicit in his five characteristics of thought is his denial of unconscious experience. Ten years after *The Principles of Psychology,* he called Frederic Myers's discovery of "feelings which are extra-marginal and outside of primary consciousness altogether. . . . the most important step forward that has occurred in psychology since I was a student of that science" and praised the work of Janet, Breuer, Freud, Mason, and others,[23] but in *The Principles of Psychology* he rejects the possibility of unconscious experience. The distinction between conscious and unconscious parts of an experience, he writes, "is the sovereign means for believing what one likes in psychology, and of turning what might become a science into a tumbling-ground for whimsies." James's ardent rejection of unconscious experience is significant in that it demonstrates his commitment to empiricism. Given his notion that conscious awareness is fringed with vague feelings of relations that constitute the mood or the emotional tone of a thought, James might easily have accepted the idea that the fringe is itself fringed with feelings that are wholly unconscious. To make this move, however, would limit the usefulness of introspection as a primary method for gathering psychological data; and James was not prepared to make this shift. In fairness to James it should be mentioned that it was mainly the associationists, the Kantians, and the Hegelians who believed in unconscious experience and that their arguments for the existence of unconscious experience are in fact fallacious. James refutes various associationist and Kantian arguments for unconscious experience and leaves the matter at that. Arguing with "the Hegelizers," as he calls them, is like "striking at some resisting gossamer with a club, one but overreaches one's self, and the thing one aims at gets no harm."[24]

In addition to his process view of the self, the total insulation of a thought from thoughts of another self, the feeling of relations, the fringe and "animal warmth" of a thought, the active teleological nature of thought, and the denial of unconscious experience, James's assessment of psychology in general and of his own in particular is important.

In James's estimation psychology was not a science; in 1890 it was only the "hope of a science." It was a field of interest more than a field of knowledge. This is not to say that James believed that psychologists did not know anything, but rather that all that was known was overshadowed by what was unknown and therefore subject to revision. Psychologists "knew" something about the human body, the central nervous system, and introspectionist psychologists "knew" something about human experience; but no one knew how to integrate these facts and that, in James's opinion, is what psychology is all about. It was the philosophical "mind/body problem" that prevented psychology from being a science; it was the Gordian knot that needed to be undone.

In the epilogue to *Psychology: The Briefer Course,* James concludes that psychology, as a science, must wait until a solid metaphysical basis can be found for it and that all the known "facts," both physiological and introspective, must be reconsidered in light of this metaphysics. "But at present," he maintains,

psychology is in the condition of physics before Galileo and the laws of motion, of chemistry before Lavoisier and the notion that mass is preserved in all reactions. The Galileo and the Lavoisier of psychology will be famous men indeed when they come, as come they some day surely will, or past successes are no index to the future. When they do come, however, the necessities of the case will make them "metaphysical." Meanwhile the best way in which we can facilitate their advent is to understand how great is the darkness in which we grope, and never to forget that the natural-science assumptions with which we started are provisional and revisable things.[25]

Eight years later, in the preface to the Italian translation of *The Principles of Psychology,* James iterates the same conclusion, "I confess that during the years which have elapsed since the publication of the book, I have become more and more convinced of the difficulty of treating psychology without introducing some true and suitable philosophical doctrine."[26] Psychologists can and should collect data pertaining to human experience and human physiology, but as a science psychology must wait until an adequate metaphysics has been formulated that will permit the integration of this data.

James realized that his psychology did not escape the problems of psychology in general. Like other psychologies, his floundered in the sea of metaphysical issues. Admitting this general similarity, however, James believed that his understanding of experience and of the self had special advantages that other psychologies did not. Obviously, he would not have argued against the associationists, the "mind-stuffists," the Kantians, and the others unless he thought that their views were seriously flawed. In his estimations, they either strayed from the empirical evidence or were guilty of logical mistakes. The associationists and the "mind-stuffists," for example, assume that substancelike sensations or actual atoms of experience can come together to form a single unified experience. Logically, James argues, this is not possible. Substances are defined such that they cannot come together into a meaningful whole. Besides, one does not experience individual sensations or mind-stuff grouped together: one simply experiences a complex whole. Kantians also depart from experience when they posit a transexperiential self or when they posit categories of understanding. General metaphysical difficulties notwithstanding, James felt that his view of experience and the self were, *on the whole,* less problematic than those of the other psychologists.

Ironically, the major problem he discerned with his own thought concerned his process view of the self. James writes:

We first assumed conscious "states" as the units with which psychology deals, and we said later that they were in constant change. Yet any state must have a certain duration to be *effective* at all.... Consciousness, as a process in time, offers the paradoxes which have been found in all continuous change. There are no "states" in such a thing, any more than there are factors in a circle, or places where an arrow "is" when it flies. The vertical raised upon the time-line on which we represented the past to be "projected" at any given instant of memory, is only an ideal construction. Yet anything broader than that vertical *is* not, for the *actual* present is only the joint between the past and future and has no breadth of its own. Where everything is change and process, how can we talk of "state"? Yet how can we do without "states," in describing what the vehicles of our knowledge seem to be?[27]

A process view of the self is unintelligible apart from the agency of individual units of experiences or thoughts. Something must be appropriating and disowning, welcoming and neglecting, and fighting for ends. Without individual "thoughts" there is nothing actual that can do these things.

James's dilemma is that, although *logic* requires that the self be a "chain" of thoughts, what is given in introspection is not individual thoughts but rather the on-goingness of thinking. As James remarks: "Consciousness... does not appear to itself chopped up in bits. Such words as 'chain' or 'train' do not describe it fitly as it presents itself in the first instance. It is nothing jointed; it flows. A 'river' or a 'stream' are the metaphors by which it is most naturally described."[28] James could not adopt his own process theory of the self without transgressing his prior commitment to empiricism. The fact that individual thoughts are not themselves empirically verifiable, according to James, "throws the question of *who the knower really is* wide open again" and renders his own process view "a mere provisional statement from a popular and prejudiced point of view."[29]

The Principles of Psychology is truly a great work. It is not a systematic work and its internal inconsistencies have been commented on by numerous scholars, but it is full to the brim with important insights and conceptual breakthroughs. Many of these insights—for example, the notion that relations are felt and that experience is partially self-determining —would be important ideas even if James had not employed them in his later thinking. If experience includes the experience of relations, solipsism may be refuted on empirical grounds—one may actually experience oneself as being related to other actualities. And if experience is partially self-determining, complete determinism goes against experience (everything cannot be completely determined if experience is partially self-determining). The fact that James does or does not draw these metaphysical conclusions from his analysis of experience is relevant when one is trying to understand James and his philosophy, but his analysis of experience and the implications that follow from it are interesting in their own right.

Two of James's greatest achievements in *The Principles of Psychology* are his process view of the self and, as a means to that end, his critique of the various substance psychologies of the period. His understanding of the self represents, in my estimation, a conceptual breakthrough. It is not simply another variety of substance psychology; it does away with psychic substances altogether. Ironically, James was unable to defend his view of the self even to himself. He realized that according to his analysis the self must be a series of thoughts, each in some manner really distinct from past thoughts of the same self, and yet he could not introspectively verify that individual thoughts exist. Indeed, empirical evidence showed that they did not. According to experience "thinking goes on." There is a *stream* of thoughts, not a *chain*.

Had James accepted the reality of unconscious experience he could have maintained that there are individual thoughts even though what is given in conscious awareness are not discrete thoughts. Charles Hartshorne, a contemporary philosopher who holds a process view of the self and the reality of unconscious experience, believes that there is a perfectly adequate evolutionary reason why one does not experience individual thoughts, namely, that conscious experience is limited to what is biologically important and individual thoughts have no biological importance. In Hartshorne's estimation, the fact that one does not consciously experience discrete thoughts is no more startling than the fact that one does not experience individual atoms. Neither is consciously experienced because neither is biologically significant; in fact, such conscious experiences would be biologically detrimental. In his words:

That we do not distinctly or consciously perceive atoms is not accidental. The utterly unmanageable complexity which would thus force uselessly, and far worse than uselessly, upon our notice, furnishes an altogether adequate evolutionary reason. Individual atoms are not biologically significant, hence not perceived. But likewise individual events [thoughts], even on a human level, are also insignificant for ordinary purposes, hence they too are not clearly perceived. A unit of human experience cannot occupy much more, rather less, than 1/10 of a second. But the important stages of thought or purpose which we normally need to distinguish and refer to as definite items succeed each other at a much slower rate.[30]

The existence of unconscious experience allows Hartshorne to accept a Jamesian view of the self as a chain of thoughts even though what is given in conscious experience is a stream of thoughts. To admit to the existence of unconscious experience James would have had to qualify his commitment to empiricism to some extent. Unconscious experience cannot be detected by introspection. In *The Principles of Psychology* James did not make this move. Later, of course, he was a firm believer in unconscious experience.

James's process view of the self suggests a process metaphysics. If the self, which has traditionally been regarded as a substance or more recently as a collection of substancelike sensations, is actually a series of experiences, perhaps other things that have traditionally been regarded as substances are also series of experiences. Perhaps there are only self-experiencing actualities and past experiences. James does not develop a process panpsychic metaphysics in *The Principles of Psychology*, although he does express his attraction to a panpsychic metaphysics,[31] but he does point out in *Psychology: The Briefer Course* that the natural science presuppositions are provisional and revisable things. In fact, this is his concluding comment. And in the preface to *The Principles of Psychology* he mentions that although he is uncritically accepting the position of natural science it is finally up to metaphysics to assess the adequacy of natural sciences as a way of understanding reality. James is almost alone among modern psychologists in his realization that the scientific position is simply one metaphysical option among many and that the fact that it has proved itself to be successful in some respects, even overwhelmingly successful, is no guarantee that that is the best perspective from which to view everything. It may be, as he suggests in *The Varieties of Religious Experience*, that the scientific position is only a useful fiction.

James's interests were never limited strictly to psychology. Even when he was writing *The Principles of Psychology* he was concerned with other matters. He was especially interested in religious and ethical issues. While in the midst of writing his psychology he wrote "Great Men and Their Environment" (1880), "Reflex Action and Theism" (1881), "Rationality, Activity and Faith" (1882), and "The Dilemma of Determinism" (1884). And just after the publication of *The Principles of Psychology* in 1890, he wrote "Moral Philosophy and the Moral Life" (1891), "Is Life Worth Living?" (1895), "The Will to Believe" (1896), *Human Immortality: Two Supposed Objections to the Doctrine* (1898), and *The Varieties of Religious Experience* (1902). In these works James addresses the major philosophical issues of the late nineteenth century: assuming the correctness of Darwin's evolutionary theory, is the human person free or strictly determined? And is there a God who is involved in worldly events? Never doubting that Darwin's theory was essentially correct, James affirms real individual freedom and he also holds that there is a God who is active in the affairs of the world. In this chapter I will focus primarily on those essays published in *The Will to Believe and Other Essays*.

The first four essays in *The Will to Believe and Other Essays* deal respectively with the relationship between emotion and understanding, the right to believe certain propositions under certain circumstances, and the relationship between belief and truth (or belief and verification); the fifth through eighth essays discuss the problems of moral and social philosophy; the ninth is a good-natured critique of Hegelian philosophy; and the tenth is James's appraisal of the accomplishments of psychical research and a comment on scientific mentality in general.[1] The first eight of these essays, placed virtually in reverse chronological order, stand against the background of Darwin's theory of evolution and James's early attraction to Spencer's evolutionary philosophy. The ninth essay fits somewhat oddly among the others because it does not pertain to anything scientific, but it is related to the other essays insofar as it is concerned with the existence of God and the possibility of real freedom.

As a young man James was "carried away with enthusiasm"[2] for Herbert Spencer's evolutionary materialism. In Spencer's schema, everything physical, biological, and social evolved or is evolving according to a single, fixed, progressive pattern. James, however, was troubled by Spencer's failure to explain conscious experience and by his subsequent denial of free will. Although there were other problematic aspects of Spencer's philosophy (e.g., his epistemology), it was Spencer's failure to explain these two topics that troubled James most profoundly. For James, a philosophy that could not account for experience overlooks one of the most basic facts of human existence, if not *the* most basic fact—namely, that it is experiential—and a philosophy that denies free will could not support any ethical claims.

Simply to say that conscious experience evolved out of entities that lack experience does not explain *how* this is possible. Poking fun at Spencer, James writes: "Spencer seems to be entirely unaware of the importance of explaining consciousness. Where he wants consciousness, he simply says, 'A nascent consciousness arises.'... Notice the terms 'incipient' and 'nascent.' Spurious philosophers of evolution seem to think that things, after a fashion, as it were, kind of 'growed.' "[3] To speak of "nascent" consciousness is to equivocate. For James a "not yet quite born" bit of awareness is equivalent to a "not yet experienced experience." An "experience" that is not experienced is no experience at all, and one is still left with the problem of experiential actualities evolving out of nonexperiential entities.

Without experience there can be no free will or self-determination, and without free will there can be no ethical requirements. Ethics presuppose free wills and free wills presuppose experience. In his lecture notes of 1876–1877 James links together what he judges to be Spencer's two major inadequacies:

I now express my belief that we can give no clear scientific description of the facts of psychology . . . without resorting to the inner at every step, that *active originality and spontaneous productivity* which Spencer's law so entirely ignores. . . . His law leaves out an immense mass of *mental fact.* My objection to it is best expressed by saying that in psychology he repeats the defects of Darwin's predecessors. . . . Pre-Darwinians thought only of adaptation. They made organism plastic to its environment . . . Darwin almost wholly discards this. He never means that spontaneous variations are causeless; nor that they are not fatally implied in the environment, since they and it are both parts of the same natural whole. He means to emphasize the truth that the regulator or preserver of the variation, the environment, is a different part from its producer.

Let me not be understood to undervalue the enormous part which direct adaptation, i.e., the teachings of experience, plays in mental evolution. The environment, meaning the sensible facts of our experience, is a vastly more potent agent in mental evolution than in physical. All the individual's acquisitions, properly so-called, come from it—and so, very likely, do many inheritances. . . . It is precisely because the action of the environment moulds the mind in so peculiar and distinct a way, that I object to allowing Spencer to say that it moulds it in every way.[4]

What Spencer's law leaves out, according to James, is the "active originality and spontaneous productivity" otherwise known as "free will." In James's eyes Darwin's theory of evolution not only allows for the possibility of free wills, it requires them. Without the originality and spontaneous productivity introduced by free wills, evolution would proceed at too slow a pace. Natural selection alone would take far longer to produce organisms as complex as human beings than nineteenth-century geology could justify.[5]

Two important facts that have bearing on *The Will to Believe* essays may be established from the preceding discussion. First, James's fundamental argument for free will is not scientific but moral. As a youth James was so impressed with the possibility that reality might be deterministic that for a time he was unable to do anything. It was only his belief that there may indeed be free will that saved him from his volitional paralysis. In his now-famous diary passage of April 30, 1870, James wrote: "I think that yesterday was a crisis in my life. I finished the first part of Renouvier's second *Essais* and see no reason why his definition of free will—'the sustaining of a thought because I choose to when I might have other thoughts'—need be the definition of an illusion. At any rate, I will assume for the present—until next year—that it is no illusion. My first act of free will shall be to believe in free will."[6] If actions follow from thoughts, then the ability to sustain one thought when one might have other thoughts is all that is needed to put an end to determinism. The ability to sustain one thought when one might have others and to do one thing when one might have done another means that the future is open-ended, that it is being fashioned each moment, and that each individual is at least partially responsible for which future possibilities become actual. Twelve years later, in a letter to Charles Renouvier, James wrote: "I believe more and more that free will, if accepted at all, must be accepted as a postulate in justification of our moral judgment that certain things already done might have been better done."[7] Without free will, regret and a sense of responsibility are illusory sensations. James believes that Darwin's theory of evolution provided scientific support for the reality of free will, but his major argument is that moral behavior presupposes the self-determination of free wills.

Second, James tends toward panpsychism as a way out of the difficulties he associated with materialism, especially Spencer's materialism. Convinced that Spencer's evolutionary materialism cannot account for the presence of experience (and that experience cannot be denied), James shifts towards panpsychism. Critiquing Spencer in *The Principles of Psychology*, he contends that "consciousness, however little, is an illegitimate birth in any philosophy that starts without it, and yet professes to explain all facts by continuous evolution. *If evolution is to work smoothly, consciousness in some shape must have been there at the very origin of things.*"[8] More complex types of consciousness can evolve out of less complex types of consciousness but consciousness itself cannot evolve out of nonconscious entities.[9] And in "Reflex Action and Theism" (1881), James cites idealism and panpsychism as examples of speculative philosophies that are congenial with his analysis of experience as purposive. "If anyone fears that in insisting so strongly that behavior is the aim and end of every sound philosophy I have curtailed the dignity and scope of the speculative function in us, I can only reply that in this ascertainment of the *character* of Being lies an almost infinite speculative task. Let the voluminous considerations by which all modern thought converges towards idealistic or pan-psychic conclusions speak for me."[10]

Now the earliest essay in *The Will to Believe,* "Great Men and Their Environment" (1880), deals with the social implication of belief in the free will of individuals. James argues against Spencer's position that the course of history may be explained apart from the activities of individuals. James maintains that it is the individual, and especially the "great man," who makes history; without individuals there would be neither historical advances nor declines.

Our problem is, What are the causes that make communities change from generation to generation? . . . I shall reply to this problem. The difference is due to the accumulated influences of individuals, of their examples, their initiatives, and their decisions. The spencerian school replies, The changes are irrespective of persons, and independent of individual control. They are due to the environment, to the circumstances, the physical geography, the ancestral conditions, the increasing experience of outer relations; to everything, in fact, except the Grants and the Bismarcks, the Joneses and the Smiths.[11]

In James's estimation, the personal decisions of the Grants and the Bismarcks, the Joneses and the Smiths, determine the course of history.

Drawing on the Darwinian notions of "spontaneous variation" and "natural selection," James makes a distinction between the causes that *produce* novelty and the causes that *maintain* novelty after it is produced.[12] He then uses this distinction on two levels: on the individual level it is free will that is the cause of novelty and the physical environment that either maintains or squelches it; on the societal level it is the "great men" who are the causes that produce novelty and the society that either supports it or fails to support it. In both cases, what is affirmed is the openness of the future. The future does not unfold according to a cosmic law but rather is made by individual men and women.

In "The Dilemma of Determinism" (1884), James openly links the possibility of freedom with morality. If reality consists of nothing but a plurality of actualities interacting in predetermined ways, then it is senseless to speak of the "moral life."

For the only consistent way of representing a pluralism and a world whose parts may affect one another through their conduct being either good or bad is the indeterministic way. What interest, zest, or excitement can there be in achieving the right way, unless we are enabled to feel that the wrong way is also a possible and a natural way . . . ? And what sense can there be in condemning ourselves for taking the wrong way, unless we need have done nothing of the sort, unless the right way was open to us as well? I cannot understand the willingness to act, no matter how we feel, without the belief that acts are really good and bad. I cannot understand the belief that an act is bad, without regret at its happening. I cannot understand regret without the admission of real, genuine possibilities in the world.[13]

It makes no sense to speak of morality apart from a view of reality that is open-ended.

The "dilemma of determinism," as James defined it, is that between pessimism and what he calls "gnosticism" or "subjectivism." In his estimation, optimism is not a viable alternative for the determinist *if* the determinist admits to the existence of evil. To admit that there is real evil is to imply regret—for it means that things would have been better if the evil that is present did not exist—and, for the determinist, this cannot be. *If* there is evil, one cannot be both an optimist and determinist. The consistent determinist must be either a pessimist or a "gnostic." The pessimist admits to the existence of evil; the gnostic denies it. Both positions are compatible with determinism. Unlike the optimist, the pessimist is free from contradiction because he or she regrets the whole of history not just some particular "evils." The "gnostic" or the "subjectivist," on the other hand, denies evil altogether. For the gnostic there are neither goods nor evils but only knowledge—reality is ethically neutral. "The dilemma of this determinism is one whose left horn is pessimism and whose right horn is subjectivism. In other words, if determinism is to escape pessimism, it must leave off looking at the goods and ills of life in a simple objective way, and regard them as materials, *indifferent in themselves,* for the production of consciousness, scientific and ethical, in us."[14]

The only escape from the dilemma of determinism, James maintains, is a belief in a world that is open-ended—a world in which the future is the result of free decisions in the present. James admits that pessimism and "gnosticism" are logically consistent alternatives, but in his opinion they are unsatisfactory because they violate his "moral demand." Any vision of the world that cannot satisfy this "moral demand" is unacceptable to James.

In the closing pages of "The Dilemma of Determinism," James attempts to demonstrate that a conception of the world as open-ended is not necessarily antithetical to a belief in divine providence. "The belief in free will," James contends, "is not in the least incompatible with the belief in Providence, provided you do not restrict Providence to fulminating nothing but *fatal* decrees." Using the example of a chess master competing against a novice, James maintains that the final outcome of the game may be assured despite the fact that the actual moves are not themselves already determined.[15] In this way, James suggests, there can be both real freedom and divine providence.

But here James clearly contradicts himself. What sense does it make to speak about real freedom within the context of a determined system? Keeping with James's conceit, why play the game if the winner is already assured? What difference does it make in the end if one gives careful consideration to each move or simply makes whatever move first pops into his or her head? Whatever his motivations for trying to reconcile the notion of providence with the view that the future is really open, the argument does not work. Unless the outcome of the game is actually dependent upon one's particular moves—unless the future is really open—moral life is undercut. Only if the outcome is really "up for grabs" does it make sense to regret making one move rather than another or to argue that one ought to make this move rather than that.

In the four will-to-believe essays, "Reflex Action and Theism" (1881), "The Sentiment of Rationality" (1896)—which is a slightly longer version of his essay "Rationality, Activity and Faith" (1882), "Is Life Worth Living" (1895), and "The Will to Believe" (1896), James explores the relationship between belief and understanding, the right to believe certain propositions under certain circumstances, and the relationship between belief and truth (or belief and verification). It is important to keep these three issues separate, even though James sometimes confuses them.

James's first point in these will-to-believe essays is that all experience is interpreted in light of some end. Because experience is teleological—because it is not simply passive but also active—no facet of human understanding is uncolored by beliefs and motives. This is as true of the scientific understanding of reality as it is of the religious understanding. James flatly rejects the notion that scientific knowledge is based solely on the facts. "As if the mind could, consistently with its definition, be a reactionless sheet at all," he exclaims. "As if conception could possibly occur except for a teleological purpose, except to show us the way from a state of things our senses cognize to another state of things our will desires! As if 'science' itself were anything else than such an end of desire, and a most peculiar one at that! And as if the 'truths' of bare physics in particular, which these sticklers for intellectual purity contend to be the only uncontaminated form, were not as great an alteration and falsification of the simply 'given' order of the world, into an order conceived solely for the mind's convenience and delight, as any theistic doctrine possibly can be!"[16] Apart from the scientific purpose and the belief that nature is uniform, science is impossible.

James's contention is not that all experience is *only* a manifestation of one's beliefs, although he has often been understood in this way, but rather that one's beliefs affect one's experience. Even the belief "that one ought not to allow his or her beliefs to enter into one's experience" is a belief that enters into one's experience. There is no escaping the teleological nature of experience.

James's second point in these essays grows out of his first point. If all experience is teleological, i.e., shaped by beliefs, one's beliefs are important. Moreover, because thoughts are at least partially self-determining, one is free to believe one thing rather than another (though one is not free not to believe anything). Under certain circumstances this freedom entails a responsibility and therefore it ought to be thought of as a "right." The "right to believe" is a conscious decision to believe one proposition rather than another. Originally James refers to this as the "duty to believe." After Chauncy Wright convinced him that this was a misuse of the term "duty," James coins the phrases the "will to believe" and later the "right to believe." The concept, however, remains the same. Under certain circumstances one is free to choose to hold one belief rather than another *and one is responsible for the decision that he or she makes.* In "Is Life Worth Living?" he writes, "we are free to trust at our own risk anything that is not impossible, and that can bring analogies to bear in its behalf"; and in "The Will to Believe" he says, "we have the right to believe at our own risk any hypothesis that is live enough to tempt our will."[17] It is necessary *that* one believes something, but *what* one believes is determined, at least at certain times, by oneself and therefore one is responsible for one's beliefs.

The "right to believe" only pertains when a decision is "forced" and "momentous" and when it concerns "live options." By "live" James means capable of being believed by the individual who is confronted with the decision. Decisions that are not forced need not be made, nor do forced decisions that are not momentous or whose options are not "live." But when a decision is forced and momentous and presents live options, a conscious decision is required; for indecision amounts to a decision against the proposition.

James's primary example of the "right to believe" is in the choice between believing that God exists and therefore that there is a moral order in the universe or believing that no God exists and that the world is morally neutral. In "The Will to Believe" he argues that because God might exist and because God either exists or does not exist and because it would be of paramount importance if God did exist, one has the right to believe that God exists. In "The Moral Philosopher and the Moral Life," James makes a similar case for the existence of a moral order, an order that presupposes God as the creator of that order. Of course one also has the right to believe that God does not exist and that morality is simply a human invention. Quoting Fitzjames Stephen, James says, "If a man chooses to turn his back on God and the future, no one can prevent him; no one can show beyond reasonable doubt that he is mistaken. If a man thinks otherwise and acts as he thinks, I do not see that any one can prove that *he* is mistaken. Each must act as he thinks best; and if he is wrong, so much the worse for him."[18] The right to believe allows for religious faith but it does not demand it.

James's third point in his will-to-believe essays is that in some cases one's beliefs may make something true that otherwise might not have become true. There is a certain class of truths, he contends, whose existence is contingent upon the beliefs and actions of human individuals. "The desire for a certain kind of truth . . . brings about that special truth's existence. . . ." At times James is quite clear about where belief in a fact may help create the fact believed in and where it cannot. "In our dealings with objective nature we obviously are recorders, not makers, of truth. . . . Throughout the breadth of physical nature, facts are what they are quite independently of us." Outside of "objective nature," however, one's beliefs may help create the fact believed in.

James gives two types of examples of belief that may create its own truth: matters concerning personal relations and matters concerning meaning or worth. The belief that someone will become a friend may be a crucial factor in that person's actually becoming a friend. Without the belief and the actions that follow from the belief, the friendship might not occur. Likewise, the belief that one will be successful in business or in sports may help bring about success. These are examples that James gives in "The Will to Believe." In "Is Life Worth Living?" James suggests that the belief that one's life is worthwhile may actually make it worthwhile. "Believe that life *is* worth living," he says, "and your beliefs will create the fact."[19]

To maintain that *in some cases* the belief in a fact may help create the fact, or more exactly, that the actions that follow from a particular belief may help create the fact believed in, is not unusual. Many people have thought this. What would be unusual would be the contention that *in all cases* one's belief creates the fact believed in. Some individuals understood this to be James's position. In particular they thought that James was contending that if one believes that there is a moral order in the universe or if one believes that God exists, then there is in fact a moral order (or will be) and God exists. What James says, however, is this: "I confess that I do not see why the very existence of an invisible world [a moral order] may not in part depend on the personal responses which any one of us may make to the religious appeal. God himself, in short, may draw vital strength and increase of very being from our fidelity. For my own part, I do not know what the sweat and blood and tragedy of this life mean, if they mean anything short of this."[20] The existence of a moral order may "in part" depend on the beliefs of individuals and God might "draw vital strength and *increase of very being*." To say that one's beliefs and actions might increase God's being is not to say that God's existence depends upon one's beliefs and activities. Indeed, it presupposes that God exists; if God did not exist it would be impossible for God to be increased by anything.

The matter of the moral order is exactly the same. In "Moral Philosophy and the Moral Life," an essay that James considered to be very important, James concludes that it is necessary for the moral philosopher to postulate the existence of God.

The stable and systematic moral universe for which the ethical philosopher asks is fully possible only in a world where there is a divine thinker with all-enveloping demands. If such a thinker existed, his way of subordinating the demands to one another would be the most appealing; his ideal universe would be the most inclusive realizable whole. If he now exists, then actualized in his thought already must be that ethical philosophy which we seek as the pattern which our own must evermore approach. In the interests of our own ideal of systematically unified moral truth, therefore, we, as would-be philosophers, must postulate a divine thinker and pray for the victory of the religious cause.[21]

If there is a moral order in the universe, it is the order that results from God's evaluation of the relative value of things. A moral order requires a divine perspective. According to this view, the *existence* of a moral order is not dependent upon the beliefs of individual human beings. If God exists, a moral order exists. However, insofar as God may draw strength and increase in being from the beliefs and actions of human individuals, the moral order may *in part* depend upon beliefs. To construe James as saying that the belief in God or the belief in a moral order in itself insures God's existence or the existence of a moral order is to misconstrue James in a very serious manner. He maintains that one has the right to believe that God exists and therefore that there is a moral perspective because it is possible and because it is a forced decision and because it is a momentous decision with "live options"; *and* in addition to this, he maintains that God might draw strength and increase in being when individuals believe that God exists and act accordingly. These are two separate contentions.

James's essay, "What Psychical Research Has Accomplished" (1890), is significant for a number of reasons: it restates his conviction expressed in his will-to-believe essays that all experience is interpreted, it presents another statement of his dissatisfaction with the traditional scientific view of the world and his own inclination toward panpsychism, and it contains his endorsement of unconscious experience. His major thesis is that traditional scientists ignore the facts that run counter to their beliefs whereas the psychical researchers, because of their beliefs, attend to all the facts. Traditional scientists would have one believe that they simply observe facts. Nothing could be further from the truth, according to James. Because they *believe* that paranormal experiences are impossible, traditional scientists do not consider the evidence. The disagreement between traditional scientists and psychical researchers is not a matter of different interpretations of the same facts, but rather a matter of different beliefs as to what are the facts to be interpreted. James is also concerned with pointing out the limitations of traditional scientific beliefs, but his major concern is with pointing out that science is based on beliefs.

James does not explicitly mention a panpsychic position in this essay, but he moves in that direction. "The only complete category of our thinking, our professors of philosophy tell us, is the category of personality, every other category being one of the abstract elements of that. And this systematic denial on science's part of personality as a condition of events, this rigorous belief that in its own essential and innermost nature our world is a strictly impersonal world, may, conceivably, as the whirligig of time goes round, prove to be the very defect that our descendents will be most surprised at in our own boasted science, the omission that to their eyes will most tend to make *it* look perspectiveless and short." He cautions against a wholly unchecked romanticism that might resemble "Central African Mumbo-jumboism"[22] but he contends that some movement toward animism or panpsychism is desirable. The impersonal materialism of traditional science is simply not adequate.

It is also significant that he reverses his earlier judgment that all experience is conscious and endorses Frederic Myers's theory of unconscious experience. In James's opinion the vast array of data collected by psychical researchers is best explained by accepting the existence of unconscious experience. Each experience—and consequently each self—is more encompassing than that small bit that is conscious and the slightly larger portion that is marginally conscious. In *The Varieties of Religious Experience*, unconscious experience is viewed as central to his explanation of "religious experiences" and in *A Pluralistic Universe* it is unconscious experience that allows for the possibility that experiences that are consciously separate may in fact be together. In fact, unconscious experience is so crucial a concept in James's later works that it is easy to forget that he denied it in *The Principles of Psychology*.

The Will to Believe and Other Essays is a collection of essays written during and just after the writing of *The Principles of Psychology*. In these essays James focuses his attention on his wider concerns: the questions of free will, the existence of God, and the status of morality. These questions lead him into other questions, most notably, the relationship between belief and understanding, the right to believe certain propositions under certain circumstances, the relationship between belief and truth. He is also interested in the social implications of free will and in psychical research. At first glance it may seem that these issues are not closely related. In his preface to *The Will to Believe and Other Essays* he tries to relate the essays on the basis of "radical empiricism" (in this case meaning the position that reality is pluralistic and open-ended) and the legitimacy of religious faith. He might have been more specific in his preface. What he ought to have said is that individual experiences are partially determined and partially free —that is to say, partially self-determining—and that this fact relativizes all knowledge, makes the individual person at least partially responsible for his or her beliefs, and makes certain events in the future contingent upon the beliefs and actions of present individuals; and that therefore the truth about those events is contingent upon the beliefs and actions of present individuals. Each of the essays points to one or more of these three conclusions that result, at least partially, from the "freedom" of experience to determine itself.

James's critique of sociological determinism is predicated on his conviction that each individual is free. Historical events come about largely because certain individuals freely decide to do one thing rather than another. "Society" is a description of how various individuals have chosen to exercise their various degrees of self-determination. It is the individuals, especially the great individuals—the bright, the powerful, the learned—who determine society, not the reverse.

James's conviction that one can make one's life worthwhile by believing it is worthwhile or that one can help bring about success in business or sports by believing that one is or will be successful is simply a corollary to his conclusion that the future is open-ended. One's future self, the person that one will be at some time in the future, is not yet determined. In part, but only in part, what one does now determines what one will become. Because each experience is influenced (i.e., partially determined) by past experiences of the same self, one's present experience plays a role in determining who one will be in the future. Believing that one's life is worthwhile or believing that one will be successful affects who one will be in the future. It does not guarantee that in the future one's life will be worthwhile or that one will be successful, but it increases the likelihood.

James's critique of traditional science and his defense of religious beliefs stem from his conclusions that all knowledge is relative and that one is finally responsible for what one believes. Scientific knowledge is not knowledge without suppositions. It is not a mere reporting of objective facts. Scientists presume that nature is similar to a machine, that it follows certain fixed laws, and that what cannot be strictly quantified is meaningless. Scientists *believe* these things just as strongly as religious individuals *believe* that God exists, that there is an objective moral standard, and that salvation is possible (if not already assured). In James's words: "We all, scientists and non-scientists, live on some inclined plane of credulity. The plane tips one way in one man, another in another; and may he whose plane tips in no way be the first to cast a stone!"[23] Not all beliefs are equally valid. Some beliefs are more correct than others. However, James's major point is not that religious beliefs are more correct than scientific beliefs; his point is rather that science does not exist apart from certain beliefs.

Freedom entails responsibility. Because science and religion offer competing beliefs and because an individual is free to decide what to believe, the individual is responsible for his or her beliefs. If one chooses to believe as a scientist believes, one is responsible for that decision. If one chooses to believe as a religious person believes, one is responsible for that decision. Responsibility cannot be avoided. One cannot escape being responsible for one's belief by choosing not to believe anything. Nonbelief is not an option. Choosing not to accept the religious beliefs is no different in its effects from choosing to accept scientific beliefs, and choosing not to accept scientific beliefs is no different in its effects from choosing to accept religious beliefs.

The fact that James fails to provide a clear framework within which to place each of the essays in *The Will to Believe and Other Essays* and the fact that he sometimes confuses logically separate issues do not invalidate his conclusions. If experience is partially self-determining—i.e., free from being completely determined by factors other than itself—then all knowledge is perspectival, individuals are at least partially responsible for their beliefs, and certain events in the future (and therefore the truth about those events) are contingent upon the beliefs and actions of present individuals. Unless one can refute the premise that experience is to some extent self-determining or free, one must accept James's conclusions.

In *Human Immortality: Two Supposed Objections to the Doctrine, The Varieties of Religious Experience,* and *A Pluralistic Universe,* James develops his understanding of God and God's interaction with human individuals. Although each of these works has its own focus, the issue that James alludes to in the preface of *The Will to Believe and Other Essays,* namely, the issue of whether reality is finally one thing or a plurality of things, plays an important role in each of these subsequent works.

One of the liveliest debates in philosophy at the turn of the century centered on the issue of whether reality is ultimately unitary or plural, or more precisely, whether there is finally only one actuality or a multiplicity of actualities. Those who believed that there is only one actuality were "monists"; those who believed that there is more than one actuality were "pluralists." In England metaphysical monism was enunciated by F. H. Bradley, in Germany by the Hegelians, and in America by James's colleague and close friend, Josiah Royce. James is usually regarded as a pluralist; indeed, he entitles his Hibbert Lectures, *A Pluralistic Universe*. However, James is not a pluralist through and through. He is attracted to some of the implications of metaphysical monism, and at times he himself endorses a type of metaphysical monism. Any interpretation of James's thought that overlooks his attraction to and his partial acceptance of metaphysical monism is too simplistic.

Not all monists agree upon the nature of the one real thing (nor do all pluralists agree upon the nature of the many actualities). Despite their differences, however, all monists (insofar as they are logically consistent) necessarily share certain general doctrines because they all agree that there is only one actuality. For example, a metaphysical monist is logically compelled to maintain that there is ultimately no duality between "subjects" and "objects." Not to do so would be to admit to dualism. For the metaphysical monist "everything" is implicit in or involved in "everything else"—there are no gaps or divisions. Ethically, a metaphysical monist is forced to contend that everything is as it must be. What appears to be evil or bad is as necessary to the whole as what appears to be righteous or good. Everything is as it "ought to be" because everything that is is necessary to the one final actuality. Freedom, the ability to introduce real novelty into the world, cannot exist. To say that there is real freedom in the world means that the future is open, that the future might be one way rather than another, and this would contradict the notion that everything is as it must be. If everything is as it must be, freedom must be denied (or be "redefined" to mean something else). Religiously, metaphysical monism entails complete unity with God. If God exists, or if one identifies God with the all-inclusive single actuality, as many monists do, then "everything" that exists exists in God (and vice versa). Although James is attracted to the religious implication of metaphysical monism and, from time to time, to its epistemological implication, he is always opposed to its ethical implications. Because he is attracted to some of its implications and adamantly opposed to others, James's rejection of metaphysical monism is never as consistent or complete as it could have been. Or, to restate this in terms of pluralism, because James is attracted to some of the implications of metaphysical monism, his "pluralism" is not as complete and consistent as it could have been. Indeed, I will argue that what James refers to in *A Pluralistic Universe* as pantheism's "pluralistic subspecies" is not intelligible as a form of pluralism at all.

In this chapter I will elaborate on James's attraction to some of the religious implications of metaphysical monism and present a careful analysis of his argument for "pluralistic pantheism" in *A Pluralistic Universe*. I will also offer my evaluation of James's success in his endeavor to frame a pluralistic alternative to metaphysical monism in *A Pluralistic Universe*.

While writing his Gifford Lectures in 1900, James comments to Royce in a letter: "You are still the centre of my gaze, the pole of my mental magnet. When I write, it is with one eye on the page, and one on you. When I compose my Gifford Lectures mentally, it is with the design exclusively of overthrowing your system, and ruining your peace."[1] Much of the rest of James's philosophy is also written with "one eye on Royce" and because of this, many scholars have come to regard James and Royce as being poles apart in every respect. James, it is thought, is a pluralist through and through and

Royce is a monist. Although James *says* and *does* much to support this opinion, in point of fact, his opposition to metaphysical monism *is* always limited to certain of its implications. In his Ingersoll Lecture, "On Human Immortality" (1889), *The Varieties of Religious Experience* (1902), "Final Impressions of a Psychical Researcher" (1909), and *A Pluralistic Universe* (1910), James endorses, or tends to endorse, one of the basic tenets of metaphysical monism, namely, that individual human selves are continuous with each other in a higher consciousness that may be referred to as "God."

In his Ingersoll Lecture, "On Human Immortality," James suggests that human brains might serve to transmit a more general experience into particular "individual" conscious experiences rather than to produce such conscious experiences. If this is the case, he contends, a whole class of experiences that are difficult to explain by a production theory of conscious experience—experiences such as religious conversion, apparitions at time of death, or clairvoyant visions—can be easily accounted for. According to James, "All such experiences, quite paradoxical and meaningless on the production-theory, fall very naturally into place on the other [the transmissive] theory.[2] Our so-called individual experiences, he hypothesizes, might be continuous in a "mother-sea" of experience. "We need only suppose the *continuity of our consciousness* with a mother-sea, to allow for exceptional waves occasionally pouring over the dam."[3] James subsequently realizes that this theory sounds like metaphysical monism and in the preface to the second edition of these lectures he clearly states that he is "anything but a pantheist of the monistic pattern" and that the transmissive theory of conscious experience might be held in conjunction with extreme pluralism. According to James: "The plain truth is that *one may conceive the mental world behind the veil in as individualistic a form as one pleases, without any detriment to the general scheme by which the brain is represented as a transmissive organ.* . . . If the extreme individualistic view were taken, one's finite mundane consciousness would be an extract from one's larger, truer personality, the latter having even now some sort of reality behind the scenes."[4] The transmissive theory of conscious experience does not demand monistic pantheism or metaphysical monism but it does support it, especially when one talks about a "mother-sea" of experience.

In *The Varieties of Religious Experience* (1902), James does not mention the transmissive theory of conscious experience per se, but he is convinced that *"the conscious person is continuous with a wider self through which saving experience comes. . . ."*⁵ Using the concept of the unconscious "more" James contends: "The further limits of our being plunge, it seems to me, into an altogether other dimension of existence from the sensible and merely 'understandable' world. Name it the mystical region, or the supernatural region, whichever you choose. . . . God is the natural appellation, for us Christians at least; for the supreme reality, so I will call this higher part of the universe by the name God."⁶ The further limits of one's personal experience are continuous with God.

As in the second edition of his Ingersoll Lectures, James takes some pains to point out how his position in *The Varieties of Religious Experience* differs from absolute monism, or what he calls "universalistic supernaturalism." According to James, the difference centers on the activity of "God." For the universal supernaturalist, God is not causally efficacious in the world—God is not the source of miracles and providential leadings. God does not *do* anything, but rather God is the point of view or perspective from which the natural world can be understood.

For them the world of the ideal [God] has no efficient causality, and never bursts into the world of phenomena at particular points. The ideal world, for them, is not a world of facts, but only of the meaning of facts; it is a point of view for judging facts. It appertains to a different "-ology," and inhabits a different dimension of being altogether from that in which existential propositions obtain. It cannot get down upon the flat level of experience and interpolate itself piecemeal between distinct portions of nature, as those who believe, for example, in divine aid coming in response to prayer are bound to think it must.

James is not totally opposed to this understanding of God, but he wants to expand it to allow God to act. For James, God is both an inclusive whole, and as such a medium of communion, *and* a causal agent. Commenting on the transcendentalists, who must be classified as "universal supernaturalists," he writes: "Transcendentalists are fond of the term 'Oversoul' but as a rule they use it in an intellectualist sense, as meaning only a medium of communion. 'God' is a causal agent as well as a medium of communion, and that is the aspect which I wish to emphasize."⁷ This is not the place to examine the intelligibility of James's claim that God is both a "medium of communion"—an "Over-soul"—and a causal agent, that human individuals are continuous with God and yet possess a degree of autonomy, but it is important to note that despite his disagreement with the "universal supernaturalists" James shares their belief that the human individual is continuous with the divine reality.

James's most extended discussion on the relative merits of monism and pluralism is found in his Hibbert Lectures, which were subsequently published under the title of *A Pluralistic Universe*. When James was invited to deliver the lecture series he was not altogether eager to accept. He was sixty-five years old, his health was failing, and he was anxious to write a tightly reasoned philosophy text; nevertheless he agreed to give the lectures. In a letter to F. C. S. Schiller he explained his decision.

I accepted because I was ashamed to refuse a professional challenge of that importance, but I would it hadn't come to me. I actually *hate* lecturing; and this job condemns me to publish another book written in the picturesque and popular style when I was settling down to something whose manner would be more *strengwissenschaftlich*, i.e., concise, dry, and impersonal. My free and easy style in "Pragmatism" has made me so many enemies in academic and pedantic circles that I hate to go on increasing their number, and want to become tighter instead of looser. These new lectures will have to be even looser; for lectures *must* be prepared for audiences; and once prepared, I have neither the strength to re-write them, nor the self-abnegation to suppress them.[8]

Unfortunately, James's assessment of his "free and easy style" and the "looseness" of his position is all too accurate.

In *A Pluralistic Universe* (1910), James reaffirms his earlier conclusion that the human individual is continuous with the divine reality. He speaks of them as "overlapping" actualities. Each conscious self, he contends, is surrounded by an unconscious "more" which in turn forms the "margin" of a superhuman intelligence, i.e., the Over-soul or God, with whom the individual conscious self may be coconscious if the threshold of consciousness is sufficiently lowered. "The *absolute* is not the impossible being I once thought it. Mental facts do function both singly and together, at once, and we finite minds may simultaneously be coconscious with one another in a superhuman intelligence."[9] James's remark that "we finite minds may simultaneously be coconscious with one another *in* a superhuman intelligence" (my emphasis) makes it quite clear that he equates being "continuous with a superhuman intelligence" with being "in a superhuman intelligence." Diagrammatically, James's position in *A Pluralistic*

Universe may thus be represented, with all of God filled up with overlapping selves:

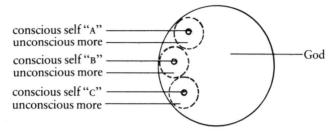

conscious self "A"
unconscious more
conscious self "B"
unconscious more
conscious self "C"
unconscious more

God

For the metaphysical monist everything is a part of the one finally real thing. Although James is adamantly opposed to the ethical implications of metaphysical monism, he is very much attracted to the notion that each individual, whether he or she is consciously aware of it or not, exists in God. In my estimation, James's religious attraction to the idea that individuals exist in God is in direct tension (at least as he formulated it) with his philosophical commitment to pluralism. Metaphysical pluralism cannot exist apart from a doctrine of external relations and it is no easy trick to have a doctrine of external relations between confluent actualities. In *A Pluralistic Universe* James seeks to construct a pluralism in which there are both internal and external relations, but he is not entirely successful.

A close reading of *A Pluralistic Universe* will reveal two very similar arguments for "pluralistic pantheism." The first of the two arguments runs like this:

(1) One's philosophy is a reflection of one's temperament.
(2) "It is normal . . . to be sympathetic [with reality]," which is to say most people are naturally inclined to demand intimate relations with the universe.
(3) Monistic pantheism—metaphysical monism or absolutism—allows for greater sympathy with the universe than does materialism.
(4) Pluralistic pantheism allows for greater sympathy with the universe than does monistic pantheism.
(5) The logical and epistemological arguments for monistic pantheism are not compelling.
(6) The "problem of evil" constitutes a major argument against monistic pantheism.

Therefore,

(7) One is free to follow his or her natural inclinations and endorse pluralistic pantheism.

The second argument is similar.

(1) "Men are once and for all so made to prefer a rational world to believe in and to live in."
(2) "Rational" or "reasonable" means the "maximal degree" of intellectual, aesthetic, moral, and practical sense.
(3) Pluralistic pantheism makes more moral and practical sense than monistic pantheism.
(4) Intellectual sense cannot override experienced fact.

Therefore,

(5) Pluralistic pantheism is "on the whole more reasonable and satisfactory"[10] than monistic pantheism.

One is immediately struck by the obvious subjectivism of the first argument's initial premise, "One's philosophy is a reflection of one's temperament," and the slightly less obvious subjectivism of the second argument's initial premise, "Men are once and for all so made to prefer. . . ." In the introduction I concluded that statements such as these ought not to be taken literally in that they undermine James's overall philosophy. Therefore, I will examine these arguments quite apart from their subjective orientation.

The key terms in the first argument are "normal" and "sympathetic nature." By "normal," James means both the statistical majority and normative. The first meaning is clearly intended in the passage, "The majority of men are sympathetic. Comparatively few are cynics. . . ." and the second meaning in the statement, "It is normal, I say, to be sympathetic in the sense in which I use the term. Not to demand intimate relations with the universe, and not to wish them satisfactory, should be accounted signs of something wrong." James was not so naive as to believe that everyone is basically the same type of person, nor was he so intolerant as to believe that everyone ought to be the same type of person—indeed, he took much delight from his acquaintances who were not normal—but he does believe that most people "ought to be" and are what he terms "sympathetic." By "sympathetic" he means inclined to believe that "the intimate and human must surround and underlie the brutal." A sympathetic person is one who desires a vision of reality in which the world is not cold, mechanical, and indifferent, but rather, warm, alive, and supportive of human endeavors. The sympathetic person requires a vision of reality in which aesthetical and moral concerns are not simply superficial but rather essential. For the sympathetic individual, "The inner life of things must be substantially akin . . . to the tenderer parts of man. . . ." The sympathetic person sees the universe as a "common *socius*" of internally motivated, responsible, interacting, beings.[11]

The key term in the second argument is "rational" or "reasonable." By "rational" or "reasonable," James means the optimal degree of intellectual, aesthetic, moral, and practical sense. In his words, "Rationality has at least four dimensions, intellectual, aesthetic, moral, and practical. . . ." The rational judgment or view is the one that allows for "the maximal degree *in all these respects simultaneously*."[12] James does not go on to discuss the relative weights of intellectual, aesthetic, moral, and practical concerns but, as will become clear shortly, moral and practical concerns are in James's opinion intrinsically weightier. Moral and practical merits being equal, intellectual and aesthetical considerations tip the balance between two visions of reality. But seldom (if ever) is this the case. The most aesthetically pleasing and intellectually consistent philosophies do not, in James's opinion, make as much moral and practical sense as philosophies that are less elegant and less consistent.

Once one recognizes what James means by the terms "normal," "sympathetic," and "rational," it becomes clear that the two arguments in *A Pluralistic Universe* are actually two forms of the same argument. The basic argument in *A Pluralistic Universe*, the one lying beneath the two arguments stated above, is this:

(1) The majority of people are, and ought to be, primarily moral and practical beings.
(2) (Materialism cannot support moral behavior.)
(3) Monistic pantheism cannot encourage moral behavior.
(4) The epistemological and logical arguments for monistic pantheism are not compelling.
(5) The "problem of evil" constitutes an important argument against monistic pantheism.
(6) Pluralistic pantheism stands as a viable philosophical position.
(7) Pluralistic pantheism encourages moral behavior.
(8) Pluralistic pantheism provides an escape from the "problem of evil."

Therefore,

(9) Most people ought to be pluralistic pantheists rather than (materialists or) monistic pantheists.

This is not a tight argument for pluralistic pantheism but it is a sound one if the conclusion follows from the premises and if all the premises are true.

The first premise, "The majority of people are, and ought to be, primarily moral and practical beings," must be granted for the sake of argument. James's point is that most people, most of the time, are motivated by what is "right" and "wrong" and by what "works" and "does not work," rather than by what is "logically consistent" and what is "logically inconsistent," or by what is "aesthetically pleasing" and what is "not aesthetically pleasing." One may wish to take exception to his added statement that this is not only the way it is but the way it *ought* to be, but there would be little point in that because the argument would be valid even without his normative judgment.

The second premise—that materialism cannot support moral behavior, is quite straightforward and unproblematic. If the world is nothing but bits of matter blindly obeying physical laws, it makes no sense to speak about what one ought or ought not do. Things will be as they will be independent of anything one does or fails to do.

The third, fourth, and fifth premises are much more problematic. These three premises constitute James's "attack on the Absolute." Each of these must be considered in some detail. Of the three, James devotes the least amount of space to the third premise, i.e., that monistic pantheism cannot encourage moral behavior. This, however, is not a good indication of the relative importance of this notion for James, because this is his major objection to metaphysical monism. He raises this objection in "The Dilemma of Determinism" (1884), in his lecture "Pragmatism and Religion" (1907), and in numerous other places. Indeed, when James summarizes his position in *A Pluralistic Universe,* he emphasizes the moral difference between pluralism and monism. "Here, then, you have the plain alternative, and the full mystery of the difference between pluralism and monism. . . . The alternative is definite. It seems to me, moreover, that the two horns of it make pragmatically different ethical appeals—at least they *may* do so, to certain individuals."[13] By "different ethical appeals" James means that monistic pantheism appeals to peace and security while pluralistic pantheism appeals to adventure, "real losses and real gains," and responsibility. In his lecture, "Pragmatism and Religion," James asks:

Suppose that the world's author put the case to you before creation, saying: "I am going to make a world not certain to be saved, a world the perfection of which shall be conditional merely, the condition being that each several agent does its own 'level best.' I offer you the chance of taking part in such a world. Its safety, you see, is unwarranted. It is a real adventure, with real danger, yet it may win through. It is a social scheme of co-operative work genuinely to be done. Will you join the procession? Will you trust yourself and trust the other agents enough to face the risk? . . ."

. . . There is a healthy-minded buoyancy in most of us which such a universe would exactly fit. . . .

Most of us, I say, would therefore welcome the proposition and add our *fiat* to the *fiat* of the creator. Yet perhaps some would not; for there are morbid minds in every human collection, and to them the prospect of a universe with only a fighting chance of safety would probably make no appeal. . . .

So we see concretely two types of religion in sharp contrast. Using our old terms of comparison, we may say that the absolutistic scheme appeals to the tender-minded while the pluralistic scheme appeals to the tough.[14]

In *A Pluralistic Universe* he makes a similar point:

Probably the weightiest contribution to our feeling of the rationality of the universe which the notion of the absolute brings is the assurance that however disturbed the surface may be, at bottom all is well with the cosmos—central peace abiding at the heart of endless agitation. This conception is rational in many ways, beautiful aesthetically, beautiful intellectually (could we only follow it into detail), and beautiful morally, if the enjoyment of security can be accounted moral. Practically it is less beautiful; for . . . in representing the deepest reality of the world as static and without history, it loosens the world's hold upon our sympathies and leaves the soul of it foreign. Nevertheless it does give *peace,* and that kind of rationality is so paramountly demanded by men that to the end of time there will be absolutists, men who choose belief in a static eternal, rather than admit that the finite world of change and striving, even with a God as one of the strivers, is itself eternal.[15]

Admitting that monistic pantheism is aesthetically and intellectually beautiful (he does *not* say intellectually sound), James qualifies his assessment of its moral reasonableness with the condition, "If the enjoyment of security can be accounted moral." This is an extremely important qualification because for the most part, if not totally, James associates the feeling of peace and security with the view that what one does or fails to do does not matter. In a world where what one does makes a difference, in a world where it makes sense to speak of moral obligations, peace and security are emotions seldom, if ever, enjoyed.

James's fourth premise concerns the epistemological and logical arguments for monistic pantheism. What I am calling the "epistemological argument for monistic pantheism" is the contention that the knower and the known must be and always have been coimplicit in each other. James deals with this argument using the proverb, "A cat may look at a king." For the monist, the fact that a cat may look at, that is, know, a king means that that king is part of what that cat is and always has been and, conversely, that being known by that cat is part of what it means to be that king. Quoting Josiah Royce, James states: "If the king can be without the cat knowing him, then king and cat 'can have no common features, no ties, no true relations; they are separated, each from the other, by absolutely impassable chasms. They can never come to get either ties or community of nature; they are not in the same space, nor in the same time, nor in the same natural or spiritual order.' "[16] For the monist, if one thing exists outside of another, knowledge is forever impossible—an entity can only be known if it exists internally to the knower. Building on this notion, the monist argues that the only coherent universe is one in which everything exists internally to everything else.

What I am calling the "logical argument for monistic pantheism" is similar but more inclusive. The logical argument has to do with relations in general, not simply the relations of knowing and being known. At the heart of the logical argument for monistic pantheism is the assumption that all relations are of the subject/predicate type, and that, to use Bradley's terminology, all relations are "internal relations."

The [epistemological] question runs into the still more general one with which Mr. Bradley and later writers of the monistic school have made us abundantly familiar—the question, namely, whether all the relations with other things, possible to a being, are pre-included in its intrinsic nature and enter into its essence, or whether, in respect to some of these relations, it can *be* without reference to them, and, if it ever does enter into them, does so adventitiously and, as it were, by an afterthought. This is the great question as to whether "external" relations can exist.[17]

If essences are eternal and if relations to other things qualify essences, then the only kind of coherent universe possible is a monistic one; for if anything exists that does not qualify and is not qualified by every other essence, it constitutes a universe of its own. This is simply the general case for which the epistemological example mentioned above is a particular case.

In James's estimation, neither the epistemological nor the logical argument is compelling. However, rather than presenting a single alternative to the more encompassing matter of relations in general and then applying it to the specific case of epistemological relations, he presents one alternative to the epistemological argument and another to the logical one. As an alternative to the epistemological argument that knowing requires that the knower and the known be coimplicit in each other, James offers his process-panpsychic hypothesis. "If we are empiricists and go from parts to wholes," he contends, *"we believe that beings may first exist and feed so to speak on their own existence, and then secondarily become known to one another."*[18] According to James, there is no reason to conclude that everything that is potentially knowable must exist within each potential knower. If one is an empiricist, one is free to hold the more realistic position that prior to being known by another being, an object may "feed so to speak" on its own existence and then subsequently exist as known to another. Or, to express this position in terms of external and internal relations, an object may first exist externally to all potential knowers and then, at some later point in time, exist as known—that is to say, exist internally to all its knowers. In James's opinion, one can accept the judgment that in some very literal sense, known objects exist internally to their knowers without concluding that they have *always* existed internally to those knowers. The epistemological position that the object known exists internally to the knower does not compel one to endorse monistic pantheism.

James's critique of the logical argument for monistic pantheism is much more extensive than his critique of the epistemological argument and is much better known. Indeed, James did not develop his process-panpsychic hypothesis in *A Pluralistic Universe* at all. He simply states that such an alternative account of knowing is possible from the empiricist perspective. According to James, the flaw in the logical argument for monistic pantheism is the assumption that actual things conform to the rules of subject/predicate logic—the logic of identity or what he terms "intellectualistic logic." In James's mind, there is no reason to suppose that actual things are like logical subjects whose only relations are predicated relations, and there are many reasons to suppose that such is not the case. In logic, a subject is precisely and eternally what it is defined (i.e., predicated) as being. In actuality, things are temporal and ambiguous, or at least seem to be. To say that actual entities are similar to logical subjects, in James's estimation, is to commit the sin of "vicious intellectualism." "Vicious intellectualism" is the systematic denial of the actual in favor of the abstract; because abstract concepts are absolutely discrete, vicious intellectuals mistakenly view the actual facts of the world as forever disjointed.

Drawing on Henri Bergson's critique of intellectualism, and especially his analysis of time, James argues that the fundamental units of actuality are not separate but "overlap" and "copenetrate." In James's words: "Past and future . . . conceptually [or intellectually] separated by the cut to which we give the name of present, and defined as being the opposite sides of the cut, are to some extent, however brief, copresent with each other throughout experience. The literally present moment is a purely verbal supposition, not a position; the only present ever realized concretely being the 'passing moment' in which the dying rearward of time and its dawning future mix their lights." Generalizing from this analysis of time, James concludes that if the past and the future—which as concepts exclude one another—coexist in a single actual occasion, there is no reason to deny that other conceptually opposite traits cohere in a single instance. Presence need not exclude absence, unity need not exclude plurality, independence need not exclude dependence, "mine" need not exclude "yours," and so forth. The principle of identity—the law that states that a thing is just what it is, a that-and-no-other—he concludes, applies only to concepts. In actuality, a thing can be both what it is and what it is not simultaneously. For James, "whatever is real is telescoped and diffused into other reals . . . [and] every minutest thing is already its Hegelian 'own other,' in the fullest sense of the term."[19] The logical argument for monistic pantheism carries no weight for James because he believes that it is a result of vicious intellectualism.

In addition to his belief that the epistemological and the logical arguments for monistic pantheism are not compelling, James is convinced that the so-called problem of evil constitutes a major argument against monistic pantheism. This is what I am calling the fifth premise of his argument for pluralistic pantheism. To claim, as the monistic pantheists must claim, that the whole of things or the Absolute is good, cannot, James contends, be reconciled to the presence of real evil in the world.

[Monistic pantheism] . . . leaves us wondering why the perfection of the absolute should require just such particular hideous forms of life as darken the day for our human imaginations. If they were forced on it by something alien, and to "overcome" them the absolute had still to keep hold of them, we could understand its feeling of triumph, though we, so far as we were ourselves among the elements over-come, could acquiesce but sullenly in the resultant situation, and would never just have chosen it as the most rational one conceivable. But the absolute is represented as a being without environment, upon which nothing alien can be forced, and which has spontaneously chosen from within to give itself the spectacle of all that evil rather than a spectacle with less evil in it. Its perfection is represented as the source of things, and yet the first effect of all that perfection is the tremendous imperfection of all finite experience. In whatever sense the word "rationality" may be taken, it is vain to contend that the impression made on our finite minds by such a way of representing things is altogether rational.[20]

If the whole of things, the Absolute, is good, why is there real evil? In James's eyes, the presence of real evil renders the hypothesis of the Absolute "decidedly irrational."

Altho the hypothesis of the absolute, in yielding a certain kind of religious peace, performs a most important rationalizing function, it nevertheless, from the intellectual point of view, remains decidedly irrational. The *ideally* perfect whole is certainly that whole of which the *parts also are perfect*—if we can depend on logic for anything, we can depend on it for that definition. The absolute is defined as the ideally perfect whole, yet most of its parts, if not all, are admittedly imperfect. Evidently the conception lacks internal consistency, and yields us a problem rather than a solution. It creates a speculative puzzle, the so-called mystery of evil and of error. . . .[21]

Unless one is willing to discount real evil as only apparent evil —a move that James would not accept—one cannot hold the Absolute to be both all-inclusive and entirely good; and if it is not all-inclusive, it is not absolute.

James's sixth premise—that pluralistic pantheism is a viable philosophical position—is absolutely crucial to his argument because, if pluralistic pantheism is not viable, then the conclusion that one ought to be a pluralistic pantheist is not sound. Pluralistic pantheism includes the notion that two things may be both separate and together *at the same time*. More exactly, it is the position that "finite minds" may be, at the same time, separate from each other and confluent in a higher consciousness. Speaking as a pluralistic pantheist, James avers, "The absolute is not the impossible being I once thought it. Mental facts do function both singly and together, *at once,* and we finite minds may simultaneously be coconscious with one another in a superhuman intelligence."[22] The same two instances of actuality may function, according to James, both separately and together—may be both external to and internal to each other—simultaneously.

James based his opinion that any two instances of actuality may be both external to and internal to each other at the same instance on the assumption that "what is true . . . of successive states must also be true of simultaneous characters." Agreeing with Bergson's assessment that the past and the future are somehow present in each present moment, James concludes that contemporary events must also somehow be present in each other. He makes the transition from successive to contemporary events in the following passage:

> In *principle,* then, the real units of our immediately-felt life are unlike the units that intellectualist logic holds to and makes its calculations with. They are not separate from their own others, and you have to take them at widely separated dates to find any two of them that seem unblent. Then indeed they do appear separate even as their concepts are separate; a chasm yawns between them; but the chasm itself is but an intellectualist fiction, got by abstracting from the continuous sheet of experiences with which the intermediary time was filled. It is like the log carried first by William and Henry, then by William, Henry, and John, then by Henry and John, then by John and Peter, and so on. . . .
>
> What is true here of successive states must also be true of simultaneous characters. They also overlap each other with their being.[23]

James does not explain *why* what is true of successive states must also be true of contemporary states, he simply asserts that it must be.

This assumption—that what is true of successive events must also be true of contemporary events—is the cornerstone of James's pluralistic pantheism. If it is an erroneous assumption, as I believe it to be, pluralistic pantheism falls apart. To my mind, there is no reason why what is true of successive events *must* also be true of contemporary events. Even if one weakens the assertion to claim, "What is true of successive states *may* also be true of contemporary states," one is at a loss to find examples where this seems to be the case. One may point to the "experience-of-the-past-in-the-present" and to the "anticipation-of-the-future-in-the-present" but are there examples of "two-separate-experiences-experiencing-together" that one can also point to? I think not. Indeed, if *two* things could be both separate from each other and, at the same time, not separate, in what sense are they actually separate things at all? A philosophy based on the premise that what is true of successive events is also true of contemporary events is finally a form of metaphysical monism.

James's seventh and eighth premises—that pluralistic pantheism encourages moral behavior and that pluralistic pantheism provides an escape from the problem of evil—are immediately suspect once one is convinced that pluralistic pantheism is not a viable philosophic position. Nonetheless, they cannot be ignored if one is involved in explicating James's case in *A Pluralistic Universe*. James's contention that pluralistic pantheism encourages moral behavior stands as the counter claim to his assertion that monistic pantheism undercuts the notion of human responsibility. Because for the monistic pantheist everything that was, is, and will be is necessary for the whole, it makes no sense to talk about what one "ought to do." Moral responsibility presupposes real freedom—it presupposes that what one does or does not do makes a difference—and in a philosophy where everything is necessary, this freedom is nonexistent. For the pluralistic pantheist this is not the case, or so James claims. In James's mind, the pluralistic aspect of pluralistic pantheism allows for the freedom and hence the moral responsibility that is lacking in a monistic pantheism. A universe in which there is a plurality of actualities, each with a degree of autonomy, would be a universe in which each actuality would be accountable for how it chooses to act in relation to other actualities. Had James argued simply for qualitative monism and *quantitative* pluralism (a pluralism of ontologically similar things), he would have been on solid ground. However, in *A Pluralistic Universe* James is not simply arguing for quantitative pluralism but for pluralistic pantheism, and one cannot separate these two aspects of his position. A thoroughgoing pluralism could support moral behavior but a "pluralistic pantheism"—a pluralism that allows for two things to be both together and separate at the same time—cannot, because it is not really a pluralism at all.

James's eighth premise—that pluralistic pantheism provides a means of avoiding the traditional problem of evil—inherits the general problem associated with pluralistic pantheism and introduces an additional problem of its own. The "general problem" of pluralistic pantheism, as I conceive it, is that it is not pluralistic at all. How can there be a real pluralism if everything is in God or, to put it in reverse, if God is not *all*-inclusive, how can one speak of *pan*theism? "Pan," after all, means "all." Quantitative pluralism and quantitative monism are contradictory notions. In addition to inheriting this general problem of pluralistic pantheism, the eighth premise introduces the problematic assumption that to be included in another consciousness is to be thereby controlled. This assumption is nowhere clearly articulated, but it is apparent in the following passages:

The believer is continuous, to his own consciousness, at any rate, with a wider self from which saving experiences flow in. . . . We inhabit an invisible spiritual environment from which help comes, our soul being mysteriously one with a larger soul whose *instruments* we are.[24]

Everything you can think of, however vast or inclusive, has on the pluralistic view a genuinely "external" environment of some sort or amount. Things are "with" one another in many ways, but nothing *includes* everything, or *dominates* over everything.[25]

For James, being included in God suggests being "instruments" of God or being "dominated" by God.

This assumption, which to my mind is totally unwarranted, forces James into the issue of theodicy. If everything is included in God, and if inclusion entails control and therefore responsibility, then God is responsible for the evil that exists. James "solves" this problem by simply assuming that not everything is in God, that God is limited either in power or knowledge or both. "The only way to escape the paradoxes and perplexities that a consistently thought-out monistic universe suffers from . . . —the mystery of the "fall" namely, of reality lapsing into appearance, truth into error, perfection into imperfection, of evil, in short . . . —the only escape, I say, from all this is to be frankly pluralistic and assume that the superhuman consciousness, however vast it may be, has itself an external environment, and consequently is finite."[26] Because he assumes that inclusion entails control and hence responsibility, James has to assume that God is not all-inclusive. Otherwise, he would be forced to conclude that God is responsible for evil.

From a process perspective, however, there is no reason to suppose that inclusion entails control. Had James been consistent in his position that events first happen and are *for themselves* and are only subsequently *for others,* he would have realized that being included in another does not constitute being controlled, because the inclusion takes place only after the included event has been determined. An event is first determined by itself and by events in its past and then it is included in other events. In terms of the "problem of evil" this means that there is no need to limit God's knowledge because being included in another experience is not to be thereby controlled.[27] This view will be discussed at greater length in chapter 5.

The conclusion of James's argument, that most people ought to be pluralistic pantheists rather than materialists or monistic pantheists, is valid—that is, it follows from his premises. But the argument is not sound because not all the premises are true. Even if one is willing to concede James his initial premise—that the majority of the people are and ought to be primarily moral and practical beings—the premise that pluralistic pantheism is a viable alternative to monistic pantheism (premise 6) and the premises that presuppose this (premises 7 and 8) are not true, as I have shown. Despite his excellent critique of monistic pantheism, James fails in *A Pluralistic Universe* to make a case for pluralistic pantheism.

In my estimation, it is as important to speculate on why James fails in *A Pluralistic Universe* as it is to recognize his failure. In my opinion, James's failure here is more technical than substantive. When I say that, I mean that there is nothing wrong with his pluralistic contention that "each part of the world is in some ways connected, in some other ways not connected with its parts, and the ways can be discriminated"[28] but he lacks the technical means of discriminating between the ways in which things are connected and the ways in which they are not. Technically, he held that the same things may be both confluent and separate *at the same time.* Had he not assumed that what is true of successive events must also be true of contemporary events he could have discriminated the ways in which things are connected and the ways in which they are not along temporal lines—things are connected insofar as present actualities include past actualities and are not connected insofar as they are contemporaries. James sought to establish a middle way between the complete disunion of all things and their complete union, or, to put it in terms of relations, he sought to discover an alternative to the position that all relations are external relations and the position that all relations are internal relations. Unfortunately, his technical position in *A Pluralistic Universe,* that things are simultaneously connected and separate, is not satisfactory.

It ought to be noted that I am not the first person to object to James's monistic tendencies in *A Pluralistic Universe* and that, when confronted with the fact that pantheism necessarily implies monism, James states that this is not what he intended. In 1910, Julius Goldstein, a German pragmatist and admirer of James, apparently pointed out to him that pluralism and pantheism are not compatible positions. James's response to Goldstein is that: "Apropos of 'pantheism,' the opposition I had in mind in that first lecture [of *A Pluralistic Universe*] was that between the divine as an *immanent* principle and as an *external* creator. In contrasting 'theism' with 'pantheism' the words suggest the numerical opposition of dualism and monism, which confuses the reader. Possibly you may find a way, in translating [*A Pluralistic Universe* into German] to mitigate the confusion."[29] James says that what he wants to assert is that God is related to the world by being *in* the world—by being in experience, but he does not mean to suggest that God is coextensive with the world, as the term pantheism indicates. James's statement to Goldstein is illuminating. James is mistaken, however, if he believes that his position is confused only linguistically. He did not know how to formulate the position he says he means to assert.

Still, there are other places in James's philosophy where he tends toward monism and these places cannot, I believe, be explained simply as technical mistakes. For example, in his article, "Final Impressions of a Psychical Researcher," written at approximately the same time as *A Pluralistic Universe,* he contends:

Out of my experience . . . one fixed conclusion dogmatically emerges, and that is this, that we with our lives are like islands in the sea, or like trees in the forest. The maple and the pine may whisper to each other with their leaves, and Conanicut and Newport hear each other's foghorns. But trees also commingle their roots in the darkness underground, and the islands also hang together through the ocean's bottom. Just so there is a *continuum of cosmic consciousness,* against which our individuality builds but accidental fences, and into which our several minds plunge as in a mother-sea or reservoir. Our "normal" consciousness is circumscribed for adaptation to our external earthly environment, but the fence is weak in spots, and fitful influences from beyond leak in, showing otherwise unverifiable common connection.[30]

Although James said that he was out to "scalp the Absolute," and was stridently opposed to many of the implications of absolute monism, he was attracted to the notion that, finally, everything (at least every human being) is included in God. It is this aspect of absolute monism that makes it impossible for James to refute absolute monism absolutely.

James's pragmatic theory of truth is famous, despite the fact that there is virtually no agreement among scholars as to its proper interpretation. A. J. Ayer and Ralph Ross believe that James's theory of truth is "anti-realistic" (Ayer's term),[1] Morton White and John Wild believe it is nonrealistic, and Edward C. Moore, H. S. Thayer, and John E. Smith believe that it is basically realistic. I think that Moore, Thayer, and Smith are essentially correct—that James's pragmatic theory of truth is a confused form of the realistic or correspondence theory of truth. In "The Will to Believe" James says: "But in our dealing with objective nature we obviously are recorders, not makers of truth. . . . Throughout the breadth of physical nature facts are what they are quite independently of us. . . ."[2] I think that James never gave up this realistic understanding of truth, though he tried to expand and clarify his position. In the preface to *The Meaning of Truth* he writes: "Altho in various places in this volume I try to refute the slanderous charge that we deny real existence, I will say here again, for the sake of emphasis, that the existence of the object, whenever the idea asserts it 'truly' is the only reason in innumerable cases, why the idea does work successfully."[3]

If one assumes, then, that James intends his pragmatic theory of truth to be realistic (that in every case, rather than "in innumerable cases," the existence of the object, whenever the idea asserts it "truly," is the only reason that the idea is true), one must account for the fact that he said "in innumerable cases" and not "in every case" and also for his other non- or antirealistic statements. In this chapter I will deal in some detail with those Jamesian comments that have misled many of the best interpreters of James's thought. There are at least four categories of misleading remarks: statements that support F. C. S. Schiller's understanding of truth; statements that truth is what it is "known as"; statements that do not clearly differentiate between truths about past facts that are already settled and "truths" about future facts that are not settled; and statements that deny the existence of propositions.

James's support of F. C. S. Schiller's "Humanism" is quite understandable. Like James, Schiller is involved in a battle with the English absolutists, Bradley, McTaggart, and Green. Moreover, Schiller stresses the volitional and subjective aspects of knowing and he is pro-evolutionary and explicitly anti-Kantian. Desperately seeking an ally and agreeing with Schiller on these important issues, James assumes that Schiller is a realist. Unfortunately, this assumption is incorrect. Unlike James, Schiller is not opposed to idealism, he is only opposed to absolute idealism.

In Schiller's estimation the absolute notion that reality and the truth about reality are already somehow complete and transhuman ignores the basic Protagorian insight that the human individual is the measure of all things. According to Schiller the human individual is "the only natural starting-point, from which we can proceed in every direction, and to which we must return. . . ."[4]

To remember that Man is the measure of all things, i.e., of his whole experience-world, and that if our standard measure be proved false all our measurements are vitiated, to remember that Man is the maker of the sciences which subserve his human purposes; to remember that an ultimate philosophy which analyzes us away is thereby merely exhibiting its failure to achieve its purpose, that, and more that might be stated to the same effect, is the real root of Humanism, whence all its auxiliary doctrines spring.[5]

Schiller is opposed to absolute idealism not because it is idealistic but because it is absolutist.

For Schiller, reality and truths about reality are human constructs. What passes for reality and for truths about reality are determined by human needs and human limitations. Time and space, external realities, physical laws, and so forth are human artifacts. They reflect human efforts to order human experience, to make it manageable. Schiller, like Kant, dismisses the possibility of knowing something in-itself. But

Schiller disagrees with Kant on two important matters; first, Schiller holds that the present categories of understanding have evolved and that new ones are evolving, and second, Schiller sees no need to talk about things-in-themselves; in his mind the "ding-an-sich" was simply a limiting concept and not a final reality.[6]

James, who had long been opposed to absolutism and to Kantism, is all too eager to side with Schiller against the absolutists and against Kant. Following Schiller's lead James makes statements such as:

Truth thus means . . . the relation of less fixed parts of experience (predicates) to other relatively more fixed parts (subjects); and we are not required to seek it in a relation of experience as such to anything beyond itself.[7]

and

Our nouns and adjectives are all humanized heirlooms, and in the theories we build them into, the inner order and arrangement is wholly dictated by human considerations, intellectual consistency being one of them. . . . We plunge forward into the field of fresh experience with the beliefs our ancestors and we have made already; these determine what we notice; and what we notice determines what we do; what we do again determines what we experience; so from one thing to another, altho the stubborn fact remains that there is a sensible flux, what is *true of it* seems from first to last to be largely a matter of our own creating. . . .[8]

But James's agreement with Schiller is always qualified. James has no intention of denying the existence of independently existing actualities nor does he mean to contend that truths are in no way connected to these actualities.[9] All James's endorsements of Schiller and all his adoptions of humanistic notions must be understood in light of his mistaken belief that Schiller is a metaphysical realist. In his review of Schiller's *Humanism*, James writes:

Grant . . . that our human subjectivity determines *what* we shall say things are; grant that it gives the "predicates" to all the "subjects" of our conversation. Still the fact remains that some subjects are there for us to talk about, and others are not there; and that farther fact that, in spite of so many different ways in which we may perform the talking, there still is a grain in the subjects which we can't well go against, a cleavage-structure which resists certain of our predicates and makes others slide in more easily.[10]

What can and cannot be said about a thing is to some degree determined by the thing itself. This is James's position and this is what he understood to be Schiller's position as well. In his article, "Professor Hebert on Pragmatism" (1908), James remarks: "Some readers will say that, although *I* may possibly believe in realities beyond our ideas, Dr. Schiller, at any rate, does not. This is a great misunderstanding, for Schiller's doctrine and mine are identical, only our expositions follow different directions."[11] But in a letter dated January 4, 1908, he writes:

Dear Schiller,

. . . I got back a week ago from the meeting at Cornell University of the Philosophical Association. . . . Your name was in many mouths, no one persuadable that you could possibly admit an "objective" reality. I, being radically realistic, claimed you to be the same, but no one believed me as to either of us. Wouldn't you subscribe to the paper I enclose [The Meaning of Truth]? Isn't the ulē [substance] which you speak of as the primal bearer of all our humanized predicates, conceived by you epistemologically as an independent *that* which the *whats* qualify, and which (in the ultimate) may be decided to be of any nature whatsoever? I hope so; for that position seems to me invulnerable. . . .

And then he makes the curious comment: "Don't answer me too minutely; if tempted to do so refrain; *I only want* to be able to quote you as agreeing [my emphasis]. If you don't agree, the bare fact [of your disagreement] suffices. . . ."[12] James found it almost impossible to entertain the possibility that Schiller did not believe in "independent thats."

James thought he and Schiller differed only in their approaches, that Schiller's approach was psychological whereas his was epistemological. But what he assumes to be merely a methodological difference is actually a difference in metaphysics. For Schiller, at least in this phase of his philosophy, there were no independent objective facts.

That the Real has a determinate nature which the knowing reveals but does not affect, so that our knowing makes no difference to it, is one of those sheer assumptions which are incapable, not only of proof, but even of rational defense. It is a survival of a crude realism which can be defended only, *in a pragmatist manner,* on the score of its practical convenience, as an avowed fiction. On this ground and as a mode of speech we can, of course, have no quarrel with it. But as an ultimate analysis of the fact of knowing it is an utterly gratuitous interpretation.[13]

Schiller was not a metaphysical realist.

Given James's mistaken assessment of Schiller's position, James's repeated claims that he and Schiller are in complete agreement cannot be accepted at face value. Although both James and Schiller oppose absolute idealism, stress the subjective aspect of experience, and are anti-Kantians, they have a fundamental disagreement concerning the existence of independent actualities.[14]

The fact that James wrongly believes that the difference between his own position and Schiller's position is only methodological has played a major role in obscuring the realistic basis of James's pragmatism. But unlike Schiller, James is an ontological realist. In his words: "My mind was so filled with the notion of objective reference that I never dreamed that my hearers would let go of it; and the very last accusation I expected was that in speaking of ideas and their satisfactions, I was denying realities outside [of human experience]."[15]

A second factor that makes James's pragmatic theory of truth appear anti- or nonrealistic is his tendency to identify truth with knowledge. "If you call the object of knowledge 'reality,' " he contends, "and call the manner of its being cognized 'truth,' cognized moreover on particular occasions, and variously by particular human beings . . . , it seems to me that you escape all sorts of trouble."[16] Identifying truth with what it is known as by particular people on particular occasions only complicates matters. Knowledge depends upon being known, it changes, and it is largely subjective. Truth, however, at least for a realist, is not dependent upon being known, does not change, and is not subjective.[17] James's identification of truth with "the manner of its being cognized" makes his theory of truth appear nonrealistic when in fact it is not. A careful reading of his position reveals that James sees himself as adding to the realistic theory of truth, not as offering an alternative to it. When pressed, James admits that truth exists independent of and prior to being known. The only condition that is necessary in order for a proposition to be true is that the actuality that is the logical subject of the proposition is characterized by those qualities (and on those actualities) denoted in the logical predicate.

That James confuses truth and knowledge is obvious in the following passages:

Truth is something known, thought, or said about reality. . . .[18]

True ideas are those we can assimilate, validate, corroborate and verify. False ideas are those we cannot. That is the practical difference it makes to us to have true ideas; that, therefore, is the meaning of truth, for it is all that it is known as. . . . The truth of an idea is not a stagnant property inherent in it. Truth *happens* to an idea. It *becomes* true, is *made* true by events. Its verity *is* an event, a process: the process namely of its verifying itself, its veri-*fication*. Its validity is the process of its valid-*ation*.[19]

In both these passages James equates truth with knowledge; an idea becomes *true* when it is *known*. Consider also his example of the person who, lost in the woods, finds what appears to be a cowpath. According to James the proposition that "there is a house at the end of the path" is neither true nor false. If by pursuing the idea of a house along the path the lost individuals arrive at a house, the proposition is verified—it *becomes* true. The proposition is *made* true by the act of seeing the house. If, however, following the mental image of a house does not eventually terminate in the sense perception of a house, the proposition becomes false.[20]

To say that the proposition, "There is a house at the end of this particular cowpath," is neither true nor false until someone verifies it makes perfect sense if what one means by "truth" is actually "knowledge." Short of taking someone's word for it, the only way a lost individual will ever *know* if there is a house at the end of a particular path is to go and look. If the individual should see a house, then he or she will *know* that there is a house at the end of the path; and if not, he or she will *know* that there is no house at the end of that path. Not only does this interpretation of James's example fit with the meaning of "know"—a lost individual is one who does not *know* where he or she is relative to his or her surroundings—it also agrees with James's many statements to the effect that knowledge is contingent upon experience and is made. In his words, "Knowledge of sensible realities comes to life inside the tissue of experience. It is *made;* and made by relations that unroll themselves in time."[21]

There are many other instances where James confuses knowledge and truth. It is impossible to consider each and every one of them within this chapter, but it is important to examine some of them, especially some of his most famous remarks. According to James:

Experience . . . has ways of *boiling over,* and making us correct our present formulas. . . . We have to live to-day by what truth we can get to-day, and be ready to-morrow to call it falsehood.

We store . . . extra truths away in our memories, and with the over-flow we fill our books of reference. Whenever such an extra truth becomes practically relevant to one of our emergencies, it passes from cold-storage to do work in the world, and our belief in it grows active.

Truth lives . . . for the most part, on a credit system. Our thoughts and beliefs "pass," so long as nothing challenges them, just as bank-notes pass so long as nobody refuses them. . . . You accept my verification of one thing, I yours of another. We trade on each other's truths.[22]

In the first of these quotations James seems to be saying that what was *true* today may not be *true* tomorrow—e.g., today it may be *true* that the earth is some five billion years old but tomorrow it may not be true; tomorrow some new discovery may convince the experts that the earth is only one billion years old. If this is actually what James means, and there are good reasons for saying that it is not, then James's theory of truth is *not* realistic. If today the logical subject of the proposition "The earth is some five billion years old" is actually characterized by the predicate "five billion years old," tomorrow it cannot be characterized by the predicate "one billion years old." However, if what James intends is that what is *known* today, about the earth or about anything else, might be outdated tomorrow, then certainly he is correct.

Similarly James's remarks that "we store . . . extra truths in our memories" and that "we live . . . for the most part on a credit system [of truth]" also pertain to knowledge rather than truth. Knowledge is "stored" in individual memories and recorded in various reference works and knowledge lives, for the most part, on a credit system. We accept each other's knowledge at face value; we trade on each other's knowledge. As statements about knowledge these two remarks do not run counter to a realistic theory of truth. Indeed, the realist could and would maintain that knowledge is stored and lives on a credit system. But for the realist what is stored in people's memories and in reference works may or may not be truths and we do not live on a credit system of truths. What is true is true regardless of someone's credit rating.

In addition to his many statements about truth that are actually about knowledge, some of James's statements actually are statements about truth. These statements, which are less well known than the statements that seem to be statements about knowledge, are entirely consistent with the realistic understanding that truths exist independently of, and prior to, being known. Sometimes James labels truths that exist independently of being known as "essential," "intellectual," "virtual," or "abstract." All these terms are synonymous. One ought to pay careful attention to what he says about this kind of truth.

Essential truth, the truth of the intellectualists, the truth with no one thinking it, is like the coat that fits tho no one has ever tried it on. . . . Pragmatist truth contains the whole of intellectualist truth and a hundred other things in addition.

There have been innumerable events in the history of our planet of which nobody ever has been or ever will be able to give an account, yet of which it can already be said abstractly that only one sort of possible account can ever be true. The truth about any such event is thus already generically predetermined by the event's nature; and one may accordingly say with a perfectly good conscience that it [the truth] virtually pre-exists.

I am perplexed by the superior importance that Dr. Pratt attributed to abstract trueness over concrete verifiability in an idea. . . . It [abstract trueness] is prior to verification to be sure . . . but it can hardly be that this abstract priority of all possibility to its correlative fact is what so obstinate a quarrel is about.[23]

According to James it is true (essentially, intellectually, virtually, or abstractly) that a coat of a certain size fits a woman of the same size even though it is not pragmatically or existentially (his word)[24] true until she tries it on. Likewise it is true in the same ways that certain creatures roamed this region of the earth two million years ago, if in fact they did, even though no one may ever know that they did. All that is required for a proposition to be essentially, intellectually, virtually, or abstractly true is for the object that is the logical subject of the proposition to have those characteristics indicated by the logical predicate of the proposition. In other words, what James means by essential, intellectual, virtual, or abstract truth is what the realist means by "truth."

James's discussion of truth in relation to Ursa Major or the Big Dipper is an excellent example of his tendency to confuse truth with knowledge and, at the same time, his realistic understanding that truth exists independently and prior to being known.

[Reality] seems to grow by our mental determinations, be these never so "true." Take the "great bear" or "dipper" constellation in the heavens. . . . we count the stars and call them seven, we say they were seven before they were counted. . . . But what do we mean by this projection into past eternity of recent human ways of thinking? Did an "absolute" thinker actually do the counting, tell off the stars upon his standing number tally . . . ? Were they explicitly seven . . . before the human witness came? Surely nothing in the truth of the attributions drives us to think this. They were only implicitly or virtually what we call them, and we human witnesses first explicated them and made them "real." A fact virtually pre-exists when every condition of its realization save one is already there. In this case the condition lacking is the act of the counting and comparing mind. But the stars (once the mind considers them) themselves dictate the result. The counting in no wise modifies their previous nature, and, they being what and where they are, the count cannot fall out differently. It could then *always* be made. *Never* could the number seven be questioned, *if the question once were raised.*

We have here a quasi-paradox. Undeniably something comes by the counting that was not there before. And yet that something was *always true.* In one sense you *create* it, and in another sense you *find* it. You have to treat your count as being true beforehand, the moment you come to treat the matter at all.[25]

What was always true ("always" meaning since the existence of those seven stars in Ursa Major), if it is true, is the proposition that "there are seven stars in Ursa Major." What *becomes* "true" is the knowledge that there are seven stars in Ursa Major. The quasi-paradox is no paradox at all; it is simply a confusing way of speaking.

Among the many interpretations of James's pragmatic theory of truth, H.S. Thayer's interpretation is most nearly correct. Thayer recognizes that James's pragmatic theory of truth is fundamentally realistic, i.e., that James's pragmatic theory of truth presupposes a correspondence between the object that is the logical subject of a proposition and the properties named in the logical predicate, and he also realizes that James uses the word "truth" in two different senses. He maintains that sometimes James uses "truth" to mean the agreement or correspondence of a belief or statement with the specified reality and sometimes to mean that a statement or belief is useful. Thayer terms the first meaning of truth "cognitive truth" and the second meaning of truth "pragmatic truth." According to Thayer pragmatic truth is a subset of cognitive truth.[26] All pragmatic truths are also cognitive truths, though not all cognitive truths are also pragmatic truths. In addition to being cognitively true, a pragmatic truth must first be compatible with the established body of knowledge, and second, must "work," that is lead to beneficial or satisfactory consequences and adaptations to experience. According to Thayer all James's statements to the effect that an idea becomes *true* or is *made* true by certain human actions should be understood in terms of cognitive truths becoming also pragmatic truths. *If* it is cognitively true that there is a house at the end of a particular cowpath, then and only then can it become pragmatically true as well, i.e., useful, when someone verifies it.

Thayer does not make the point that the second meaning of "truth" in James is not a new meaning of truth at all but only a confusion with knowledge. (He does, however, recognize that James confuses truth with knowledge.)[27] Knowledge first must be compatible with the established body of knowledge and second must "work." A recognition of this would require Thayer to rework his account of the relationship between "pragmatic truth" and "cognitive truth," because knowledge is not always a subset of true propositions. For example, at one time the earth was known to be flat. This knowledge was compatible with the established body of knowledge and it "worked" for hundreds of years—that is, it allowed people to navigate along the coast and to draw maps—but it was never true. Some knowledge may be true, but something need not be true in order for it to be knowledge. Thayer's account of James's pragmatic theory of truth does not explain how something that is not true ("cognitively true") can work; indeed he denies that it can. In this respect his interpretation of James's theory of truth is limited.

A third reason that James's pragmatic theory of truth sounds nonrealistic, or even antirealistic, is that James does not systematically distinguish between truths about past and present actualities and "truths" about future actualities. H. S. Thayer's analysis of James's pragmatic theory of truth does not explain this.[28] James is opposed to any understanding of truth that closes off the future. According to the absolutist theory of truth, the Truth—i.e., the final absolute truth about everything, past, present, and future—is already determined. In his eagerness to defend the doctrine that the future is not yet determined, and hence that "truths" about future actualities are not yet determined, James speaks at times as if all truths are contingent upon what happens in the present, when in fact only "truths" about future actualities are contingent upon what happens now. Truths about past and present actualities are already determined by virtue of the fact that the actualities are just what they are. Some of James's statements concerning ideas that *become* true—that are *made* true by human actions—are not based upon a confusion of truth and knowledge; they pertain instead to the openness of the future.

In 1907, Alfred C. Lane, a former pupil of James, questioned him on the nature of truths about past actualities and truths about future actualities. Lane puts forth three options: (1) the whole time-process, past and future, is rigidly determined and hence the truth about past and future actualities is determined; (2) only the past is so determined and hence only the truth about past actualities is determined; and (3) nothing is determined—all past, present, and future actualities are not determined and hence the truth about all actualities is not determined. (Logically, Lane ought to have included another option, namely, that past *and present* actualities are already determined and hence the truth about past *and present* actualities is already determined.) Lane goes on to state his position:

Now in this last horn [of the trilemma] I have no faith . . . I think the facts are against it; that is, as I understand the structure of the universe, a physicist on some fitting fixed star could today see the cohorts crucifying Christ on Calvary, or hear the bellowing of prehistoric beasts, had he instruments of sufficient delicacy, and that to sufficiently refined sensibilities the cosmos would be one echoing whispering-gallery of all past time. . . . Thus so far as the past is concerned I must, must I not, class myself as a "tender-minded softy"? *Verification means to me not making the idea true, it is making me know it to be true. Is the truth less true before it is verified? Or does its difference to me make any difference in it?* It would doubtless make a great practical difference to me as a deacon of an orthodox church if Christ did not take that walk to Emmaus. It would, so far as I know or can see, make no difference to anyone if the youngest uncles of Thotmes III had ever swam in the Nile. But *I cannot see that my life or anyone else's affects the truth of the propositions.* . . .[29]

James replies:

The second horn of the trilemma is mine, —with the future partly indeterminate while the past is given fully. The third horn (with the writhing past) I absolutely repudiate, for I can frame no notion of the past that doesn't leave it inalterable. Truths involving the past's relations to later things can't come into being till the later things exist, so such truths may grow and alter, but the past itself is beyond the reach of modification.[30]

James is quite clear that past (and presumably present) actualities are just what they are—nothing can change them, they are "inalterable" and, although he does not say so in this particular letter, what is virtually true about these actualities is already determined, even if it is not known. What James emphasizes in this letter to Lane is that some things will become true that are not already true. The relation between some particular future actuality and some particular past actuality does not exist prior to the existence of that future actuality and therefore truths involving that relation do not either, prior to that future actuality. For example, if it is true that Martin Luther King, Jr., was greatly influenced by reading Mohandas Gandhi's works, it did not become true until King read Gandhi's works. New truths come into existence when new actualities come into existence.

Some of the clearest statements concerning James's position on "truths" about future facts, though they are not as clear as they might be, are found in *The Will to Believe and Other Essays*. In these essays James speaks of "a certain class of truths" that is dependent upon the beliefs and actions of individuals.[31] The sort of "truth" that he has in mind is the "truth" of the proposition that you will be my friend. Believing that you will be my friend and acting accordingly will help make this proposition true sometime in the future. For James, a proposition regarding the future, especially those parts of the future subject to human influence, is not already true or false. It can be made true or it can be made false depending on what individuals decide in the present. This aspect of James's theory of truth is a corollary of his meliorism.

The position that the past and the present are not yet determined and, therefore, that what is true about past and present actualities is not yet determined *is* nonrealistic. But the position that only the future is open and, therefore, that what will be true in the future is not already determined, is neither nonrealistic nor antirealistic. It is confusing to speak of "truths" that are not already true and may never become true, but there is nothing in this position that puts it at odds with a realistic or correspondence theory of truth. James's failure to systematically distinguish, in his own thinking, between the truth about past and present actualities and the "truth" about future actualities leads him to speak at times as if the past and the present are really open and that one can make something true about these actualities that is not already true. For example, he writes, "odd as it may sound our judgment may actually be said to retroact and to enrich the past. Our judgments, at any rate, change the character of *future* reality by the acts to which they lead."[32] Had James been more careful in separating truths about past and present actualities and "truths" about the character of future reality, he never would have said that it is possible to change the past or to *make* something true about past actualities that is not already true. Strictly speaking, it is only "truths" about future actualities that can be made.

The fourth factor that tends to make James's pragmatic theory of truth sound non- or antirealistic is his denial of propositions. Propositions are essential to a realistic theory of truth. For the realist, "truth" denotes a certain relation between an actuality and a proposition; namely, a proposition is true if the predicate of the proposition designates qualities (and/or other actualities) that in fact inhere in the actuality that is the logical subject of the proposition. Some propositions are true, some are false. Because James formally rejects the reality of propositions, his pragmatic theory of truth appears to be unrealistic.

[handwritten marginalia: James wouldn't agree]

James gives two reasons for rejecting propositions: first, they are neither ideas nor objects; second, they are not anywhere. (The second objection is based on the realistic premise that everything that is is somewhere.) His first objection is stated most clearly in two letters written in 1908:

> *"That"* Caesar existed, e.g., is not an intermediary between the objective fact "Caesar-existed" and the other objective fact "someone's-belief-that-Caesar-existed," but a muddle of the two facts, made to appear as a medium of connection between them by granting to it the objectivity of the first fact and the truth of the second. Surely truth can't inhabit a third realm between realities and statements of beliefs. . . . The great merit of pragmatism [is] to have stepped right over all such mongrel figments [as supposals or propositions].[33]

> "Propositions" are expressly devised for quibbling between realities and beliefs. They seem to have the objectivity of the one and the subjectivity of the other and he who uses them can straddle as he likes, owing to the ambiguity of the word *that* which is essential to them.[34]

Because propositions are neither ideas (or beliefs) nor realities, James argues, they are nothing at all.

In *The Meaning of Truth* James raises his second objection. In an imagined debate with an antipragmatist, in this case a not-too-clever realist, James poses the question, Where are true propositions located prior to being entertained by someone in particular?[35] James cannot imagine how a realist might answer this and thus believes that he has dealt a great blow to the realist's position.

At first glance James's rejection of propositions would seem to indicate that his pragmatic theory of truth is not realistic. On closer examination, however, this is not the case. Once again the difference between James's position and that of the realist is a verbal confusion rather than a doctrinal difference, for James's "virtual" truths (or what he calls "intellectual," "essential," or "abstract" truths) function like true propositions. According to the pragmatic theory of meaning, then, "virtual" truths and true propositions are identical. Take for example James's statement that, in regard to the seven stars in Ursa Major, "something comes by the counting that was not there before. And yet that something was *always true*." He might just as well have said that the proposition "There are seven stars in Ursa Major" has been true, if it is true, as long as those stars have existed, even though no one knew it for billions of years; but instead he says that it was virtually true before it became known by particular individuals.

The fact that virtual truths are functionally identical to true propositions renders his first objection to propositions meaningless; virtual truths are neither ideas nor objects, and yet they exist. It should also be noted that James is not opposed to the existence of Platonic forms ("concept-stuff") even though they are neither ideas nor objects. In *Some Problems of Philosophy,* which was written at approximately the same time as *The Meaning of Truth,* he states: "What I am affirming here is the platonic doctrine that concepts are singulars, that concept-stuff is inalterable, and that physical realities are constituted by various concept-stuffs of which they 'partake.' "[36] To say that only ideas and objects exist undercuts his own notion of virtual truths and of "concept-stuff."

James's second objection, that propositions must be somewhere if they exist, however, is a valid criticism of any realist who cannot locate propositions somewhere in the universe. Of course it is also a valid criticism of James's doctrine of virtual truths and of "concept-stuffs." In his "Miller-Bode" notebooks James argues that one must posit a "cosmic omnibus" where all truths obtain. "One must admit a cosmic omnibus of 'being' for each 'experience' [actuality] in which what is true of it is realized."[37] In *The Meaning of Truth* James does not mention any such cosmic omnibus, some place where propositions (and presumably "concept-stuffs") are situated. It is not important to settle here the issue of where virtual truths or true propositions are, it is important only to point out that James's second objection to the existence of propositions is a valid objection only to those realists who cannot locate propositions somewhere in the universe.

James's explicit rejection of propositions makes his pragmatic theory of truth appear nonrealistic. In fact, however, James simply replaces the term "proposition" with his own term, "virtual truth."

Copy

James's pragmatic theory of truth, when properly understood, is a realistic theory of truth; it assumes a correspondence between a proposition and a specific actuality or group of actualities. In order to demonstrate this I have argued that James is confused in four respects—he believes that F. C. S. Schiller is a metaphysical realist; he tends to identify "knowledge" with "truth"; he fails to systematically make a distinction between truths about past and present actualities and "truths" about future actualities; and he rejects propositions (though he believes in virtual truths). James, I imagine, would consider it a dubious favor to have the realism of his pragmatic theory of truth defended by arguing that he is confused on major issues, but I think he would be pleased to have his theory of truth recognized as being realistic in any event.

How is it that James came to make so many mistakes in regard to truth? Many different explanations could be offered. In my estimation the two most important reasons are that he thought he could render the realistic theory of truth more concrete, and that he did not intend to enter into a full-length discussion on truth; he simply wanted to attack the absolutist notion of truth and subsequently, to defend himself from the slanderous charge of "idealism."

James's desire to make the realistic theory of truth more concrete accounts in large measure for his tendency to identify truth with knowledge and his denial of propositions. Knowledge characterizes ideas and beliefs and as such is more concrete than propositions. Ideas are propositions that are entertained by someone and beliefs are ideas that are held with conviction. The fact that ideas and beliefs are more concrete than propositions, however, does not mean that there are no propositions or that ideas have the same properties as propositions.

James's desire to make truth more concrete is related to his wish to do battle with the absolutist theory of truth. James is opposed to the absolutist notion that the Truth exists independently of human knowledge, but James is also opposed to the absolutist theory of truth because it holds that the Truth —meaning, the final truth about everything past, present, and future—already exists. This understanding of truth is totally unacceptable to James. He wants to emphasize that there are truths, with a small "t" and an "s," and that some truths do not already exist and that at least some of these truths are dependent upon human beliefs and actions. James assumes that this is compatible with, or a part of, the realistic theory of truth, on the basis that it is the complete opposite of the Absolute Idealist position. (He also assumes that F. C. S. Schiller is a realist primarily because Schiller opposes Absolute Idealism.) However, James is not always very clear as to which truths are fixed and independent of human beliefs and actions and which "truths" are not. When asked explicitly, James admits that "the future is partly indeterminate while the past is given fully. . . . I can frame no notion of the past that doesn't leave it inalterable," but in the heat of his polemics against the absolutist position he often posed it as an all or nothing affair: either all actualities—past, present, and future—and all truths about them are determined and independent of human actions, or none are. The realists wanted neither part of this false alternative and regarded James's pragmatic theory as alien to their own.

James rapidly grew tired of defending his pragmatic theory of truth. In his letter to Lane he remarks, "I have had such a mass of correspondence about 'Prag' lately that I am rather tired of writing on the subject. . . ." The fact that he keeps writing on truth even after he becomes weary of the subject is a testimony to his combative spirit and his conviction that his theory of truth, when properly understood, is realistic. It was difficult for James to pass up a challenge and it was even more difficult for him to suffer misunderstanding, especially when he was being called an idealist, the very position he was fighting against. Writing to Charles Strong about his (James's) theory of truth, he states: "I have always intended (though I may have made verbal slips) to be realistic, and to be called an idealist . . . makes me feel queer."[38]

All things considered, James's pragmatic theory of truth, although it is some of his best-known work, is some of his most confused. Nonetheless, the evidence is clear that his pragmatic theory of truth is basically realistic.

5   *Pure Experience and Panpsychism*

In addition to all his other interests, James turns his attention at times to pondering the fundamental nature of reality from a metaphysical standpoint. James's metaphysical thought can be divided into three periods: 1900 to 1904, 1904 to 1905, and 1905 to 1910. From 1900 to 1904 James was a panpsychist, from 1904 to 1905 he oscillated between being a phenomenist and a panpsychist, and from 1905 until his death in 1910 he was, again, a panpsychist.

Prior to 1900 James did not engage in metaphysical matters per se. In *The Principles of Psychology* and in his *Will to Believe and Other Essays in Popular Philosophy* he assumed, for the most part, the prevailing metaphysical position that there are two types of actualities: extended substances (which are devoid of mentality) and thinking things. Of course in *The Principles of Psychology* he departed from the traditional position that the "thinking things" were substances and held instead that the thinking things were simply thoughts—momentary psychic events. This departure from the traditional view has profound metaphysical implications, many of which he developed after 1900, but prior to 1900 James tended to regard his doctrine of thoughts as nothing more than a psychological theory.

James's friend and former student, Charles Augusta Strong, was in part responsible for James's endorsement of panpsychism—the metaphysical position that everything actual is, or has been, an experience for itself. Strong embraced panpsychism wholeheartedly and also encouraged James to do so. This position was especially attractive to James (and to Strong) because it could account for the natural evolution of higher forms of experience out of lower forms of experience and by doing so did not bifurcate the natural world. In *The Principles of Psychology* James commented:

The demand for continuity has, over large tracts of science, proved itself to possess true prophetic power. We ought therefore ourselves sincerely to try every possible mode of conceiving the dawn of consciousness so that it may *not* appear equivalent to the irruption into the universe of a new nature, non-existent until then.

Merely to call the consciousness "nascent" will not serve our turn. It is true that the word signifies not yet *quite* born, and so seems to form a sort of bridge between existence and nonentity. But that is a verbal quibble. The fact is that discontinuity comes in if a new nature comes in at all. The *quantity* of the latter is quite immaterial. The girl in "Midshipman Easy" could not excuse the illegitimacy of her child by saying, "it was a small one." And Consciousness, however little, is an illegitimate birth in any philosophy that starts without it, and yet professes to explain all facts by continuous evolution.

If evolution is to work smoothly, *consciousness in some shape must have been present at the very origin of things.*[1]

James was not a panpsychist when he wrote this, but he became one shortly thereafter.

In 1904–1905 James wrote a series of articles for the *Journal of Philosophy* which were later published as *Essays in Radical Empiricism*. *Essays in Radical Empiricism* contains two mutually exclusive metaphysical positions. The dominant one—the one that is usually referred to as James's "Radical Empiricism" or "Philosophy of Pure Experience"—is the view that reality is comprised of events that are intrinsically neither psychical nor physical but potentially either or both. Bertrand Russell termed this position "neutral monism"; James termed it "phenomenism." According to this position "psychical" and "physical" denote two types of relationships that events can take on relative to each other. The subordinate, and generally overlooked, position is panpsychism. According to panpsychism, the events or actualities that comprise reality are intrinsically psychical, i.e., they are or have been experiences for themselves. It is very doubtful that James consciously intended to enunciate two metaphysical positions. The fact that he used the term "pure experience" to designate the basic unit of both philosophies indicates that he meant to outline a single system. It remains, however, that sometimes a "pure experience" is inherently neither psychical nor physical and at other times a "pure experience" is an un-analyzed experience, which is to say, it is inherently psychical.

James's ambiguous use of the phrase "pure experience," coupled perhaps with the present popularity of phenomenology and the unpopularity of panpsychism, has led most of James's interpreters to the conclusion that James gave up panpsychism in 1904 and became a phenomenist. In my estimation, this conclusion disregards a host of facts. It disregards the panpsychic elements of *Essays in Radical Empiricism*, his syllabus for "Philosophy 1a" (1905–1906), his return to panpsychism in the final pages of his "Miller-Bode" notebooks in 1908, and his favorable allusions to panpsychism in *A Pluralistic Universe*, "Final Impressions of a Psychical Researcher" (1909), and *Some Problems of Philosophy* (1912). The evidence suggests that James was a panpsychist who, for a brief period of time, was interested in phenomenism and not, as most believe, a phenomenist who, for a brief period of time, was a panpsychist.

Both James's philosophies of pure experience are, to varying degrees, "process philosophies." In both his panpsychism and his phenomenism what have traditionally been regarded as enduring substances were regarded as a series of momentary events. This emphasis upon a process view of reality represents a generalization of his process view of the self in his psychology. In his *Essays in Radical Empiricism* and in his "Miller-Bode" notebooks he realized that there were definite metaphysical advantages associated with the doctrine that "objects" as well as "subjects" are actually streams or chains of events rather than enduring substances. Although he seemed to think that it was easier to wed a process view of reality to phenomenism than to panpsychism, there are many places where he linked his process philosophy with his panpsychism. I will pay special attention to the process aspects in both his panpsychism and his phenomenism and to the epistemological significance of his process panpsychism.

James's first unambiguous affirmation of panpsychism is in his "Philosophy of Nature" course ("Philosophy 3") which he taught at Harvard in 1902–1903. In his course outline he states that "pragmatism would be his method and 'pluralistic panpsychism' his doctrine," and then proceeds to explain that by "pluralistic panpsychism" he means the doctrine that "material objects are 'for themselves' also."[2] However, he clearly states the central tenet of panpsychism in his Gifford Lectures, "The Varieties of Religious Experience," which were delivered in 1901–1902. In *The Varieties of Religious Experience* he writes: "A conscious field *plus* its object as felt or thought of *plus* an attitude toward the object *plus* the sense of a self to whom the attitude belongs—such a concrete bit of personal experience may be a small bit, but it is a solid bit as long as it lasts. . . . It is a full fact, even though it be an insignificant fact; it is of the *kind* to which all realities whatsoever must belong. . . ."[3] Everything actual must be the same *kind* of thing as a moment of human experience. (Notice he says the same *"kind"* and not simply the "same." It would be foolish to say that everything actual has to be just like a moment of human experience, which itself varies from person to person and from moment to moment within the same person; but, unless one is willing to endorse a metaphysical dualism where there is more than one *kind* of actuality, one has no choice but to say that everything actual must be the same *kind* of thing as a moment of human experience.)

If everything actual is the same kind of thing as a moment of human experience, then the world view of the physical sciences is wrong, the "physical" world is not strictly physical. In *The Varieties of Religious Experience* James proffers this conclusion: "The final human opinion may, in short . . . revert to the more personal style. . . . If this were so, the rigorously impersonal view of science might one day appear as having been a temporarily useful eccentricity rather than the definitively triumphant position which the sectarian scientist at present so confidently announces it to be."[4] For James the "more personal style" does not mean animism; there is no reason to suspect that a river or a mountain, for example, is the same kind of thing as a moment of human experience. "More personal" simply means more personal than the lifeless, mechanistic view of the physical sciences.

In 1903, in his review of Schiller's book, *Personal Idealism*, James repeats his panpsychic contention that everything actual is metaphysically similar to a moment of human experience.

The only fully complete concrete data are, however, the successive moments of our own several histories, taken with their subjective personal aspect, as well as with their "objective" deliverance or "content." After the analogy of these moments of experiences must all complete reality be conceived. Radical empiricism thus leads to the assumption of a collectivism of personal lives (which may be of any grade of complication, and superhuman or infrahuman as well as human), variously cognitive of each other, variously conative and impulsive, genuinely evolving and changing by effort and trial, and by their interaction and cumulative achievements making up the world.[5]

(Again, note that James says "after the analogy of" human experience and not "identical to" and he makes a point of stressing "of any grade of complication.")

The evidence for James's being a panpsychist from around 1900 to around 1904 is rather convincing. Those interpreters of James who maintain that he was always attracted to panpsychism but never adopted such a position are, at best, guilty of misreading the evidence.

In 1904 and 1905 James published a series of articles that were subsequently published as *Essays in Radical Empiricism*. It is not easy to discern James's position in these essays; indeed, he later confessed in a letter to Strong that "in those articles I was groping and fumbling anyhow, and doubtless guilty of much confusion."[6] Most of James's interpreters have understood these essays to signal James's turn away from panpsychism. Ralph Barton Perry, James Edie, John Wild, Charles Morris, Edward Madden, and Peter Hare, to name but a few, all agree that after 1904 James was not a panpsychist (if he ever were one). What they do not agree upon is what James's metaphysical position was after 1904. Some people such as Perry, Madden, and Hare think that James was some type of metaphysical realist; others, such as Edie, Wild, and Morris, think that he was a phenomenist. At the moment, those who agree with Edie, Wild, and Morris are in the majority.

The phenomenist position that James expresses in *Essays in Radical Empiricism* is based on the principle that everything actual is an instance of a primal stuff that is inherently neither physical nor psychical. He terms this primal stuff "pure experience." In the first of these essays, "Does Consciousness Exist?" he begins: "My thesis is that if we start with the supposition that there is only one primal stuff or material in the world, a stuff of which everything is composed, and if we call that stuff 'pure experience,' then knowing can easily be explained as a particular sort of relation towards one another into which portions of pure experience may enter." "Psychical" and "physical" or "subject" and "object" denote ways in which pure experiences function in regard to other pure experiences. "On the principles which I am defending, a 'mind' or 'personal consciousness' is the name for a series of [pure] experiences run together by certain definite transitions, and an objective reality is a series of similar [pure] experiences knit by different transitions."[7]

James's phenomenism is difficult to comprehend. By way of explanation James provides several examples. One example that he gives is of a pen. In itself it is "a bald *that,* a datum, a fact, phenomenon, content, or whatever other neutral or ambiguous name you may prefer to apply"—it is a "pure experience."[8] Insofar as it functions as a physical object, e.g., holds ink, writes on real paper, remains stable over time, reacts to the impact of other "physical" objects, it is rightly classified as a physical object. Insofar as it functions as an idea, e.g., does not hold real ink, does not write on real paper, is subject to one's fancy, is impervious to the impact of "physical" objects, it is rightly classified as an idea of a pen. It is the function of a pure experience, not its inherent qualities, that determines whether it is psychical or physical.

A second example that James gives is of a room. This example is significant because James analyzes a room in precisely the same manner he analyzes a pen.

As a [physical] room, it will take an earthquake, or a gang of men, and in any case a certain amount of time, to destroy it. As your subjective state, the closing of your eyes, or any instantaneous play of your fancy will suffice. In the real world, fire will consume it. In your mind, you can let fire play over it without effect. As an outer object, you must pay so much a month to inhabit it. As an inner content, you may occupy it for any length of time rent-free.[9]

Apparently anything can be regarded as a "pure experience" —a pen, a room, a nation, the world. In his phenomenism James makes no distinction between individuals and aggregates.

In the same letter to Strong in which James confesses that he is "groping and fumbling anyhow, and doubtless guilty of much confusion," he states that in the articles that comprise *Essays in Radical Empiricism* "the problem there was metaphysical, not epistemological; it was an analysis of the *nature* of what is experienced, not of the meaning of knowing, and whatever epistemology I may have brought in was by the way, and illustrative, not fundamental."[10] Still, his position that the same pure experience may function differently in two separate contexts, at the same time, overcomes the duality of subject and object without denying the object's independent existence. James likens knowing to the intersection of two lines; at one and the same time a single point lies in two lines. According to this understanding of "know," when one knows a pen, for example, one's experience of a pen and the physical pen are the same "pure experience" functioning in two contexts at the same time. In one context the pure experience functions as a physical object, in the other context it functions as an idea. The object experienced and the experience of the object are the same neutral fact or phenomenon taken twice over.

Defined as the neutral stuff of which everything "psychical" and "physical" is composed, "pure experience" is a very odd metaphysical concept. It provides a solution to the epistemological problem of the relationship between the idea and the object known, but it is a very unrealistic solution. There is, however, a second meaning of "pure experience" in *Essays in Radical Empiricism* which is not strictly a metaphysical notion and is not at all unrealistic. The second meaning, which is not compatible with the first, is prereflective experience, or what James calls "unverbalized sensation." This second type of pure experience is "pure" in the sense that it is unanalyzed and hence not tainted by culturally specific ways of understanding. In the essay, "The Thing and Its Relations," James writes:

"Pure experience" is the name which I gave to the immediate flux of life which furnishes the material to our later reflections with its conceptual categories. Only new-born babes, or men in semicoma from sleep, drugs, illnesses, or blows, may be assumed to have an experience pure in the literal sense of *that* which is not yet any definite *what*. . . . Pure experience in this state is but another name for feeling or sensation. . . . Its purity is only a relative term, meaning the proportional amount of unverbalized sensations which it still embodies.[11]

Pure experience, in its second meaning, is an experience free from all interpretations; indeed, it is hardly conscious.

This second meaning of "pure experience" is a type of knowing. What James later calls radical empiricism's "statement of fact," that "the relations between things, conjunctive as well as disjunctive, are just as much matters of direct particular experience, neither more so nor less so, than the things themselves," assumes this meaning of "pure experience." "Prepositions, copulas, and conjunctions, 'is,' 'isn't,' 'then,' 'before,' 'in,' 'on,' 'beside,' 'between,' 'next,' 'like,' 'unlike,' 'as,' 'but,' flower out of the stream of pure experience, the stream of concretes or the sensational stream as naturally as nouns and adjectives do. . . ."[12] Not only things themselves but the relations between things are given in "pure," i.e., pre-reflective, experience.

The importance of recognizing this second meaning of "pure experience" is that it enables one to acknowledge James's commitment to "radical empiricism" without equating "radical empiricism" with phenomenism or neutral monism, for despite James's explicit affirmations of neutral monism in some parts of *Essays in Radical Empiricism* there are other places in those same essays where his ontology is clearly a form of panpsychism. Understood as prereflective experience, "pure experience" and panpsychism are compatible doctrines.

In several places in *Essays in Radical Empiricism* James enunciates the central tenet of panpsychism, viz., that everything actual is or has been self-experiencing, and, though he does not claim to be a panpsychist, speaks very highly of his panpsychist friends Henri Bergson and Charles Strong. He recognizes that there is some connection between his "radical empiricism" and their panpsychism, but he does not venture to speculate on what it might be. When discussing the status of actualities outside of anyone's experience, he writes: "The beyond must of course always in our philosophy be itself of an experiential nature. If not a future experience of our own or a present one of our neighbor, it must be a thing in itself in Dr. Prince's and Professor Strong's sense of the term—that is, it must be an experience *for* itself whose relation to other things we translate into the action of molecules, ether-waves, or whatever else the physical symbols may be." In another place he remarks that "the pure experiences of our philosophy are, in themselves considered, so many little absolutes, the philosophy of pure experience being only a more comminuted *Identitätsphilosophie*."[13] Both of these statements are just different ways of saying that everything actual is an experience for itself.

James's two references to panpsychism in *Essays in Radical Empiricism* are favorable, though he stops short of outright endorsement. After commenting that something actual that lies outside anyone's experience of it must be "an experience *for* itself," he says, "This opens the chapter on the relations of radical empiricism to panpsychism, into which I cannot enter now." It is more significant that when James comes up against the "urgent problems of activity," by which he means causal relations, he remarks that the answers to these questions "lead however into that region of pan-psychic and onto-logic speculation of which Professors Bergson and Strong have lately enlarged the literature in so able and interesting a way." He goes on to say, "The results of these authors seem in many respects dissimilar, and I understand them as yet but imperfectly but I cannot help suspecting that the direction of their work is very promising, and that they have the hunter's instinct for the fruitful trails."[14]

From 1905 to 1908 James kept a notebook as part of his effort to think through what he called the "Miller-Bode objections" to his neutral monism. Dickinson S. Miller, in several personal letters and in an unpublished manuscript, and B. H. Bode, in a series of articles, objected to the unrealistic implications of James's phenomenism. In his article, " 'Pure Experience' and the External World," Bode wrote that "the philosophy of pure experience does not account for our awareness of a world beyond our individual experience; and it also fails to show how there can be a world that is common to a multiplicity of individuals."[15] Like the neo-realists who banded together in 1910 under the leadership of Ralph Barton Perry, neither Miller nor Bode presumed to have solved the epistemological problems presented by a realistic ontology, but they were convinced that James's phenomenism "solved" the epistemological problem outside the context of ontological realism. In Bode's words:

Something will have been accomplished, if it is shown that the problems of reference to a beyond, of correspondence between individual thought-processes and reality external to them, remains a genuine problem and is not to be set aside as essentially meaningless. . . . The "beyond" to which our thought refers is not a reality identical with the fragmentary part of a present content, as Bradley contends, nor is it identical with such a content [as James contends]. . . . Whatever the nature of reference may ultimately turn out to be, there is at present no sufficient ground for the view that an adequate account of it can ever be given in terms of immediate experience.[16]

Bode thought that it was better to recognize the problem of knowing independently existing objects as a genuine problem than to "solve" the problem by calling the object "pure experience."

James was particularly receptive to these criticisms of his phenomenism presumably because of his own deep-seated commitment to metaphysical realism. To speak of rooms and pens that are intrinsically neither objects nor subjects nor someone's perception of objects as being actually anything at all is very difficult. In his syllabus for "Philosophy 1a" (1905–1906), in several places in his *Essays in Radical Empiricism,* and in his "Miller-Bode" notebooks, James returned to his panpsychism and said that things exist independently of anyone else's experience of them *because they are self-experiencing.* In his syllabus for "Philosophy 1a" he wrote:

Our only intelligible notion of an object *in itself* is that it should be an object *for* itself, and this lands us in panpsychism and a belief that our physical perceptions are effects on us of "psychical" realities. . . . *That* something exists when we as individuals are not thinking it, is an inexpungable conviction of common sense. The various stages of idealist reflection are only as many successive attempts to define *what* the something is that thus exists. The upshot tends pretty strongly towards something like panpsychism.[17]

And in his "Miller-Bode" notebooks, February 11, 1908, he wrote:

The world *is* business . . . but the "agent" (element, substance, subject) which grammar and thought require, can be expressed as the potentiality of residual business. . . . Turning to my own particular puzzle, how shall we translate all this? The "pen," as a living real, is the name of a business centre, a "firm." It has many customers, my mind, e.g., and the physical world. To call it the *same pen* both times would mean that although my mind and the physical world can and may eventually figure in one and the same transaction, they need not do so . . . and that in respect of this particular pen-experience neither *counts* in the transaction which the other is carrying on. Neither is *counted* by the other, neither is *for* the other. All such coming and going and alternation connects with the general notion of being counted, observed, associated, or ignored and left separate. These are essentially psychic expressions so that the constitution of reality which I am making for is of [the] psychic type.[18]

In each of these quotations, James's endorsement of panpsychism is manifest. The neutral events of his phenomenism gave way to self-experiencing actualities.

In addition to these passages where James is clearly espousing panpsychism, one can also point to his sympathetic references to panpsychism in *A Pluralistic Universe, Some Problems of Philosophy,* and "Final Impressions of a Psychical Researcher," an article he wrote in 1909. In *A Pluralistic Universe* he alludes to "the great empirical movement toward a pluralistic panpsychic view of the universe, into which our own generation has been drawn" which is destined to become the rival of absolute idealism.[19] In light of James's commitment to empiricism, this is a very telling comment. In *Some Problems of Philosophy* he notes that causation in the "physical world" lends itself to a panpsychic explanation: "The concrete perceptual flux, taken just as it comes, offers in our own activity-situations perfectly comprehensible instances of causal agency. . . . If we took these experiences as the type of what actual causation is, we should have to ascribe to cases of causation outside of our own life, to physical cases also an inwardly experiential nature. In other words we should have to espouse a so-called 'pan-psychic' philosophy."[20] And in "Final Impressions of a Psychical Researcher," the last article James published, he states that out of his experience as a researcher "one fixed conclusion dogmatically emerges." This conclusion is that "Our 'normal' consciousness is circumscribed for adaptation to our external earthly environment, but the fence [that surrounds it] is weak in spots, and fitful influences from beyond leak in, showing the otherwise unverifiable connection." He then says, "Not only psychic research, but metaphysical philosophy, and speculative biology are led in their own ways to look with favor on some such 'panpsychic' view of the universe as this."[21] (Perhaps he ought to have said "pantheistic" rather than "panpsychic" but panpsychic was the word he used.)

I have quoted James at such length in regard to panpsychism because so few individuals have recognized that he gave up phenomenism in favor of panpsychism.[22] Most of James's interpreters, for various reasons, have concluded that James was a panpsychist from 1900 to around 1904 and then adopted phenomenism or returned to a traditional dualistic type of metaphysical realism. I think these views overlook too much contrary evidence. James was not satisfied with the unrealistic character of his phenomenism nor was he satisfied with a dualistic realism; therefore he adopted panpsychism, a metaphysical position that is nondualistic and that may be regarded as a variety of metaphysical realism insofar as it allows for the existence of actualities independently of anyone else's experience of them.

James's phenomenism and his panpsychism are both process philosophies—both describe things "in the making." The process element of his phenomenism has already been alluded to. For the phenomenist, "subjects" and "objects" are not enduring substances, but rather they are serially ordered societies of "pure experiences." " 'Mind' or 'personal consciousness,' " James says, ". . . is the name of a *series of experiences* run together by certain definite transactions, and an objective reality is a series of similar experiences knit by different transitions."[23]

James's panpsychism is also, at least part of the time, a type of process philosophy.[24] In the same "Miller-Bode" notebook entry where he states "the constitution of reality which I am making for is of [the] psychic type," he writes, "At bottom it seems nothing but this . . . that neither world nor things are finished, but in process."[25] James makes similar remarks in *A Pluralistic Universe*. "The essence of life is its continuously changing character . . . ," he maintains, and "What really *exists* is not things made but things in the making."[26] In all of these passages, and in others, James enunciates or implies a process panpsychism—a process philosophy based *not* on experiencing substances, but on momentary experiences that exist in serially ordered societies.

The process element of both phenomenism and panpsychism is important in respect to epistemology. In phenomenism it is the notion that both "subjects" and "objects" are actually series of events that allows for the metaphor of intersecting lines. An object is known when a neutral event is an objective reality in one context and a mental reality in another context.

A process panpsychism permits another, more realistic, theory of knowing. The traditional problem associated with a realistic epistemology is to explain how the same object may exist independently of someone else's experience of it (i.e., outside of any knower's experience) and yet also exist as experienced (i.e., as part of some knower's experience). Using the term *"co"* to denote an object's existence *as internal to some knower* and the term *"ex"* to denote its existence *as external to any knower*, James realized that an object can be both *co* and *ex* a knower if knowing is essentially an asymmetrical relationship. If subjects and objects are actually chains of psychic events, there is no contradiction involved in holding that an object, *as it is for itself*, is *ex* a potential knower, and *co* the knower *as it is known*. James cites the example of human experience: as known (i.e., remembered) a moment of human experience exists *co* the knower (i.e., the present thought), but in itself it existed independently of being known (i.e., remembered) by the now-present moment of experience. James expresses his discovery in the following passage:

> In general terms the condition in question is only a case of non-reciprocity in relation. That at any rate is the *logic* of it. Experience presents examples of it whenever there is *direction* in the relation. Things are not *mutually* later, higher, between, etc. Remembrance is not mutual. Why need "consciousness" [knowing] be mutual? If it is not mutual, wherein lies the paradox? Apparently in the principle laid down so stoutly in my *Psychology*, that mental facts are as they appear, and can't "appear" in two ways *to themselves*. . . . [But] a mental it . . . is alive enough to carry on more than one business. It can *turn* inside of itself; which means that without ceasing to *be* itself, it can stand in many relations, of which being with the "rest" is only one. Both *ex* and *co*![27]

The paradox of something's being both *ex* and *co* another actuality is no paradox at all when seen from a process perspective. What was once *ex* may be *co* in a subsequent moment. For James, this realization had both religious and nonreligious importance. Religiously it was important because it provided a structure within which human individuals can be both internal to God—*co* God—and separate from God—*ex* God. From a nonreligious perspective it was important because it overcame the gap between the knower and the object known without undermining the reality of objects existing independently of anyone else's experience of them. In this chapter only the nonreligious aspect of this process epistemology will be considered.

The basic epistemological fact for a process panpsychic realism is the experience of another experience—the feeling of another feeling. James's example of remembrance is particularly instructive because, for the process panpsychist, it is the simplest possible case of knowing. A recent experience that existed independently of anyone else's experience of it, now exists as it is known in a subsequent experience. The experience of one's bodily experience presents a somewhat more complicated example of knowing because, unlike just past thoughts, bodily experiences are usually mediated through other bodily experiences. James makes this point in reference to his "arm-feelings": "My arm-feelings can be, though unnoticed. . . . They can also be noticed, and cooperate with my eye-feelings in a total consciousness [experience] of 'my arm.' *Your* arm-feelings can't so cooperate, presumably for lack of neural conditions."[28] My arm-feelings can be for themselves, though unnoticed by me (i.e., they may exist *ex* me) and they can be and be known by me (i.e., they may exist *co* me). Moreover, my arm-feelings may give rise to certain eye-feelings, which is to say that the self-experiencing actualities that make up my arm—the cells in my arm—may affect the self-experiencing actualities that make up my eyes—the cells in my eyes. Likewise the self-experiencing actualities that make up your arm—your arm cells—may affect my eye cells. Most, if not all, of one's experience of the external world—the world outside one's body—is experienced only indirectly, i.e., as mediated through bodily experiences such as neural experiences.

I do not mean to suggest that James ever formally developed a process panpsychic epistemology; he did not. But he did lay the foundation for this type of realistic epistemology in his "statement of fact" that experience includes the experience of relations and with his doctrine that knowing is an asymmetrical relationship in which the object known is included in the knower but not the reverse. From 1908 to 1910 James was too busy doing other things to devote his efforts to epistemological matters. On the one hand he was defending his "pragmatic theory of truth" against the charge that it was unrealistic and, on the other hand, he was attacking absolute idealism. These two tasks, both done in what James termed the "popular style," occupied the last few years of his life. There are, of course, statements in his lectures against absolute idealism that have epistemological implications, but for the most part James focused his attention in these lectures on such topics as the status of real possibilities, human effort, the "unconscious more," the existence of evil in the world and the relevance of this fact for a doctrine of God, and not on epistemology per se.

This chapter examined James's metaphysical positions from 1900 to 1910. Searching for a way to overcome the ontological and epistemological dualisms that he had adopted in *The Principles of Psychology*, James turned to doing metaphysics.

From 1900 to 1904 James thought that the most adequate philosophical position was a pluralistic panpsychism in which "material objects are 'for themselves' also." In this way the ontological or qualitative dualism between "mental things" and "physical things" is done away with. Beginning with the bit of actuality that is most accessible to human beings, namely, an instance of human experience, James reasoned that all actual things must be ontologically, or metaphysically, similar. This does not mean that each instance of actuality closely resembles a human "thought"—there may be enormous differences between one instance of actuality and another—but the differences cannot be ontological.

In 1904 and 1905 James flirted with another possibility: perhaps everything actual is comprised, not of psychic events, but of neutral events. He termed these neutral events "pure experiences." Neutral monism or phenomenism had the advantage of avoiding both ontological and epistemological dualism; however, it was a hard position to defend. In what sense is a "pure experience," which is neither for itself (i.e., psychic) or for someone else (i.e., physical), actually anything at all? And why call it an "experience"?

In his "Miller-Bode" notebooks of 1905–1908 James responded to the allegations that his phenomenism was not actually a form of metaphysical realism. In these notebooks, as well as in his "Philosophy 1a" course, James reaffirmed his panpsychism, a doctrine that is not entirely absent from his *Essays in Radical Empiricism.* To contend that every actual entity is for itself, whether it is for anything else or not, clearly puts James back on the side of the metaphysical realists. Unlike the metaphysical idealists who maintain that there are some things that exist only insofar as they are a part of someone's experience of them, the panpsychist holds that everything that exists can exist independently of anyone else's experience of it.

In several places James associates his panpsychism with the notion that everything is in process. This fact is particularly important in that it provided James with the necessary foundation for a realistic epistemology. In his "Miller-Bode" notebooks he realized that certain relations are asymmetrical or, to use his word, "non-reciprocal." This means that an actual entity that was, at one moment, for itself alone could, at a subsequent moment, be for another actual entity. James spoke of this in terms of being *"ex"* and *"co"* another being. According to this position an actuality can be for another, i.e., as it is known, only after it has been for itself. In chapter 6, I will devote more attention to process panpsychism and to James's beliefs that "relations are given in experience" and that knowing is an example of an asymmetrical relation where the object known is *"co"* the knower and the knower is *"ex"* the object known.

For all its originality and insightfulness, James's thought is
unsystematic and often confused. His pragmatic theory of
truth and his "pluralistic pantheism" are especially tangled.
Of course his philosophy may be systematized—the confusions may be resolved and the inconsistencies reconciled—
but how one systematizes it depends on what one takes to be
James's major insights and most important ideas. To my
mind James's most significant insights and his most salient
concepts are these:

(1) the self is actually a series of experiences
(2) there is a plurality of actualities
(3) the sum total of actualities is increasing
(4) to be is to be (or to have been) an experience for oneself
(5) relations are felt (and therefore ingredient in experience)
(6) to act on anything means to get into it somehow
(7) knowing is asymmetrical, and
(8) God is in some respects limited, i.e., has an environment and
    lacks the ability to control every aspect of reality.

James did not always affirm each of these eight notions, and
at times he endorsed ideas that are contrary to one or more of
these ideas; nonetheless these are the insights and the concepts that, to my mind, characterize the essence of his thought
überhaupt.

   Another philosophy that affirms each of these Jamesian
concepts is the process philosophy of Alfred North Whitehead. Whitehead, who developed his philosophy independently of James, had many of the same insights and arrived at

many of the same conclusions. But unlike James, Whitehead was a system-builder. In his book, *The Unifying Moment: The Psychological Philosophy of William James and Alfred North Whitehead,* Craig Eisendrath maintains that "scattered throughout James's work . . . is a system *in posse.* Such a scheme is developed by Whitehead."[1] By and large, I agree with Eisendrath's contention.[2] I do not think that had he lived longer James would have written a book similar to Whitehead's *Process and Reality;* in fact, I doubt that he would have appreciated it had he lived to read it. Nevertheless, Whitehead's process philosophy—his "philosophy of organism"—stands as an example of a systematic philosophy built around those very notions that I have termed James's most significant insights and most salient concepts.

The purpose of this chapter is to show how, *on Jamesian principles,* James's philosophy might have been more systematic than it is. I will focus on three main issues: what does it mean to be actual; what type or types of relations are possible between actual things; and what is the status of formal logic vis-à-vis reality. On all these matters I will draw heavily upon Whitehead's process philosophy.

What Does It Mean To Be Actual?   Whitehead is quite clear regarding what it means to be actual—only actual entities are actual. " 'Actual entities'—also termed 'actual occasions'— are the final real things of which the world is made up. There is no going behind actual entities to find anything more real. They differ among themselves: God is an actual entity, and so is the most trivial puff of existence in far-off empty space. But, though there are gradations of importance, and diversities of function, yet in the principles which actuality exemplifies all are on the same level. The final facts are, all alike, actual entities; and these actual entities are drops of experience, complex and interdependent."[3] To fully explain Whitehead's understanding of what it means to be actual would require a detailed discussion of every aspect of his philosophy of organism, because every part of his system involves every other part. Obviously, such a discussion cannot be undertaken here. Those who are interested in exploring Whitehead's metaphysics will find several very good introductions to his thought. It is, however, possible to make several observations concerning Whitehead's understanding of being actual and to say something regarding the process element of his philosophy.

First, Whitehead explicitly agrees with the Jamesian notions (2) and (4) that there is a plurality of actualities and that to be is to be (or to have been) an experience. Indeed, Whitehead knowingly employs a Jamesian phrase in stating that "actual entities are drops of experience. . . ."

Second, Whitehead is not an animist. By distinguishing between "true individuals" (e.g., electronic occasions, cellular occasions, and occasions of human experience) and "aggregates" of individuals (e.g., rocks, vegetables, and crowds), and by distinguishing between experience and conscious experience (the latter being a particular kind of the former), Whitehead avoids the admittedly implausible position that electronic occasions or mountains, for example, or single-celled organisms or chairs, are somehow conscious. For Whitehead, everything actual is self-experiencing, but some things are only aggregates of actual entities and even among actual entities only the most complex enjoy any degree of conscious experience. Whitehead's philosophy is a very sophisticated panexperientialism, but it is not a type of animism.

Third, Whitehead's panexperientialism can be viewed as a brand of metaphysical realism. To say that everything actual is (or has been) an experience for itself includes the realistic notion that things can and do exist independently of being experienced by someone or something else.

Fourth, according to Whitehead, actual entities perish as soon as they become actual. This is their droplike nature. Once an experience happens it ceases to exist *as a subject* and exists only as an object for all future subjects to take account of. Everything actual first exists as a subject for itself and then as an object for others. This is the process element of Whitehead's philosophy.

James is also a panexperientialist and a process philosopher, though not consistently so. In chapter 5, I traced his commitment to panexperientialism—or more precisely, "pan-psychism"—from his 1902–1903 statement, "material objects are 'for themselves' also," to the closing pages of his posthumously published book, *Some Problems of Philosophy*. There he writes: "If we took these experiences [human experiences of causation] as the type of what actual causation is, we should have to ascribe to cases of causation outside of our own life, to physical cases also, an inwardly experiential nature. In other words we should have to espouse a so-called 'pan-psychic' philosophy."[4] There are times, of course, when James is not a panexperientialist. He is not, for example, a panexperientialist in *The Principles of Psychology* and in most of his *Essays in Radical Empiricism*. In *The Principles of Psychology* he accepts a form of dualism in which ideas and material atoms are equally actual, though metaphysically different, and in most of his *Essays in Radical Empiricism* he professes a type of phenomenalism. Steeped in British Empiricism, James cannot easily part with the notion that an object is merely the sum of its appearances. But in *The Principles of Psychology* James wanted to stay away from metaphysical issues and in his *Essays in Radical Empiricism* he was inconsistent. In addition to his phenomenistic statements, one finds statements such as: "The beyond must . . . always in our philosophy be itself of an experiential nature. If not a future experience of our own or a present one of our neighbor, it must be a thing in itself . . . that is, it must be an experience *for* itself. . . ."[5] And in his syllabus for "Philosophy 1a," a course he taught in 1905–1906, the year after his *Essays in Radical Empiricism*, he writes:

Our only intelligible notion of an object *in itself* is that it should be an object *for* itself, and this lands us in panpsychism and a belief that our physical perceptions are effects on us of "psychical" realities. . . . *That* something exists when we as individuals are not thinking it, is an inexpungable conviction of common sense. The various states of idealist reflection are only as many successive attempts to define *what* that something is that thus exists. The upshot tends pretty strongly towards something like panpsychism.[6]

James's metaphysical realism is not consistently panexperiential, but it is panexperiential much of the time.

James is also inconsistent in his process notion that "enduring substances" are in fact serially ordered societies of events. The basis of James's doctrine of process is his theory of the self in *The Principles of Psychology*. In direct opposition to the Kantian position that the self is an enduring substance, James maintains that the "self" is a series of psychic events which he terms "thoughts" or "feelings." Each thought occurs, perishes, and is superseded and owned by another.

It is a patent fact of consciousness that a transmission like this actually occurs. Each pulse of cognitive consciousness, each Thought, dies away and is replaced by another. The other, among the things it knows, knows its own predecessor, and finding it "warm" . . . greets it saying: "Thou are *mine,* and part of the same self with me." Each later Thought, knowing and including thus the Thoughts which went before, is the final receptacle—and appropriating them is the final owner—of all that they contain and own. Each Thought is thus born an owner, and dies owned, transmitting whatever it realized as its Self to its proprietor.[7]

What Kantians took to be substance, James considered to be a serially ordered sequence of psychic events.

In *Essays in Radical Empiricism*, in his "Miller-Bode" notebooks, and in *A Pluralistic Universe*, James generalizes this concept into a doctrine pertaining to everything actual. In his "Miller-Bode" notebooks, for example, he states: "At bottom it seems nothing but this . . . that neither world nor things are finished, but in process." To say that "everything is in process" does not necessarily imply a process panexperientialism, but on a good many occasions James did link his process view with his panexperientialism. In fact, in the same notebook entry where he remarks ". . . that neither world nor things are finished, but in process," he states that "the constitution of reality I am making for is of [the] psychic type."[8]

On the issue of what it means to be actual, both James and Whitehead are of the opinion that moments of experience are, in the last analysis, the only actual things. Whitehead holds this position more consistently than James does; nonetheless, it is a position that attracts James and one that he endorses on many occasions.

What Type or Types of Relations Are Possible Between Actual Things?   Like most metaphysical realists, James maintains that the many existing actualities are related—that they affect and are affected by other actualities—although he had no theory of relations per se. "Each part of the world," he states, "is in some ways connected, in some other ways not connected with its other parts, and the ways can be discriminated."[9] In *A Pluralistic Universe*, where this statement is found, he remarks that "to act on anything means to get into it somehow" and in *The Meaning of Truth* he states that "relations are felt," or more precisely, "relations between things, conjunctive as well as disjunctive, are just as much matters of direct particular experience, neither more so nor less so, than the things themselves."[10] In themselves these two principles of relations, i.e., that to act on anything means to get into it somehow and that relations are felt, do not constitute a theory of relations. They are, however, suggestive of a theory. Indeed, they suggest a theory of relations similar to Whitehead's theory which entails both of these principles.

Apart from his confused treatment of relations in *A Plural-istic Universe* where everything is both connected and discon-nected with everything else at the same time, James does not enter into a discussion of relations in general. Rather he deals with specific types of relations or instances of relatedness in conjunction with other issues. He comments on the relation that exists between one human individual and another, the re-lation that exists between God and any given individual, the relation between the "knower" and the "known," and the re-lation between God and the world. In order to discuss James's implicit theory of relations it is necessary to consider each of these types of relations separately.

In *The Principles of Psychology, Essays in Radical Empiri-cism,* and *A Pluralistic Universe,* James addresses the matter of how one self is related to another. In *The Principles of Psy-chology* and *Essays in Radical Empiricism* James places much greater emphasis on the separateness or unrelatedness of in-dividuals than he did in *A Pluralistic Universe.* In *The Princi-ples of Psychology* he states: "Every thought tends to be part of a personal consciousness. . . . no one of them is separate, but each belongs with certain others and with none beside. My thought belongs with my other thoughts, and your thought with your other thoughts. . . . No thought even comes into direct *sight* of a thought in another personal conscious-ness than its own. Absolute insulation, irreducible pluralism, is the law."[11] And in his *Essays in Radical Empiricism* he states: "My experience and your experience are 'with' each other in various *external ways,* but mine pass into mine, and yours pass into yours in a way in which yours and mine never pass into one another."[12] In both cases, the series of "thoughts" that are my "self" and the series of "thoughts" that are your "self" exist outside one another. "Absolute in-sulation" is the final law in the relation between individuals.

In *A Pluralistic Universe,* however, James reverses himself. "The particular intellectualistic difficulty that had held my own thought so long in a vise was . . . the impossibility of un-derstanding how 'your' experience and 'mine' which 'as such' are defined as not conscious of each other, can nevertheless at the same time be members of a world experience defined ex-pressly as having all its parts coconscious, or known to-gether."[13] According to James it is only intellectualistic logic that prevents a self from being both separate from and to-gether with another self simultaneously. If one rejects the principle of identity, then any particular thought can be both what it is and what it is not—both itself and another—at the same time. Real separateness and real togetherness can and do exist simultaneously.

Whitehead agrees with James's general statement that "each part of the world is in some ways connected, in some other ways not connected with its other parts, and that the ways are distinguishable," and with his particular conclusions (5) and (6)—that relations are felt (and therefore ingredient in experience) and that to act on anything means to get into it somehow. According to Whitehead: "Actual entities involve each other by reason of their prehensions of each other. There are thus real individual facts of the togetherness of actual entities, which are real, individual, and particular. . . ."[14] More specifically, Whitehead believes that actual entities in the past exist also *in* present actual entities. Present actual entities are constituted in part of past actual entities. In respect to the relations between two human individuals, Whitehead's theory of relation may be diagrammed like this:

A $>$ $>$ $>$ $>$ $>$

B $>$ $>$ $>$ $>$ $>$

Time   1   2   3   4   5

At time$_1$ A and B are absolutely distinct. At time$_2$, however, both persons' experiences at time$_1$ have entered into their experience at time$_2$ (i.e., A_1 entered into A_2 and B_2 and B_1 entered into both B_2 and A_2). Likewise at time$_3$ both persons' then-present experiences are distinct, although each has a history that includes not only its own immediate past experience but also the immediate past experience of the other, and so on. Of course one can allow for differences in the way A_1 is felt or prehended by A_2 and the way B_1 is felt or prehended by A_2, and similarly for the way B_1 is felt by B_2 and the way A_1 is felt by B_2; but these differences are not absolute. A_1 and B_1 are both prehended by A_2 though they are prehended differently. Both of James's principles of relations are affirmed: that relations are felt, i.e., that they are matters of direct experience, and that to act upon something is to get inside it somehow. According to Whitehead's position, "All real togetherness is togetherness in the formal constitution of an actuality."[15]

Person A is able to act upon person B, to affect B, because A's past experiences are ingredient *in* B and they are *in* B because they are felt by B. For Whitehead, individuals are together in that they include each other's past experiences and separate in that they exclude each other's present experiences. Instead of saying, as James does in *A Pluralistic Universe*, that individuals are separate and together simultaneously (together on a "higher plane"), Whitehead maintains that strictly contemporary experiences are *first* separate and *then* together in subsequent experiences. There is real separateness and real togetherness, but they occur sequentially and not simultaneously.

A second type of relation that James comments on is the relation between God and a specific human being. As I point out in my third chapter, James's thinking on how God and a human individual are related is not wholly consistent. On the one hand he agrees with the absolutists that everyone exists internally to God—that each human consciousness shades off into the divine consciousness, and on the other hand, he views God and the human being as copartners in creating the future. In *The Varieties of Religious Experience* he remarks: " 'God' is a causal agent as well as a medium of communion . . ."[16] and in *A Pluralistic Universe* he writes that "the absolute is not the impossible being I once thought it. Mental facts do function both singly and together, at once, and we finite minds may simultaneously be coconscious with one another in a superhuman intelligence."[17] In these two important works James's position is that human individuals are both internally and externally related to God. One is *at the same time* both *in* God and *alongside* God and vice versa.

In *A Pluralistic Universe* James defends the apparent inconsistency of his position by rejecting the principle of identity. In his "Miller-Bode" notebooks, however, he offers another explanation. Puzzled by how the same thing can be both *"ex"* and *"co"* another thing, James realizes that not all relations are reciprocal. In relations where there is a "direction," relations are nonreciprocal. "Things are not mutually later, higher, between, etc. Remembrance is not mutual. Why need "consciousness" be mutual? If not mutual, wherein lies the paradox? . . . To take the pantheistic case, 'I' can be, and be known; be and have another being next [to] me; why can't I have another being own and use me, just as I am, for its purposes, without knowing any of these purposes myself?"[18] Although the use of the term "pantheistic" is clearly inappropriate insofar as God is "another being" and there is no reason to suppose, as James does, that "knowing" entails "using," it is evident that James believes that God and a human being can be both internally and externally related to each other *if one views both of them as temporal beings.* If God and the human being are both temporal beings, the relation that pertains to one moment of divine and one moment of human experience may be different from the relation that pertains to two other moments of human and divine experience. One moment of human experience may be internal to God and another moment of human experience *in the same self* may be external to a moment of divine experience, and vice versa. In short, James is suggesting, at least in the case of God and human individuals, a theory of relations that is identical to Whitehead's general theory of relations.

Using a diagram similar to the one used to illustrate Whitehead's account of how individual human beings interact, one can diagram James's "Miller-Bode" theory in the following manner:

God	$>$	$>$	$>$	$>$	$>$
A	$>$	$>$	$>$	$>$	$>$
B	$>$	$>$	$>$	$>$	$>$
Time	1	2	3	4	5

At time$_1$ God and the human selves, A and B, exist alongside each other. At time$_2$ the just-past experiences of persons A and B (i.e., experiences A$_1$ and B$_1$) enter into and affect what God is at that moment. Likewise, at time$_2$ persons A and B include in their experience God's experience at time$_1$. According to this view, God and the human individual are mutually immanent and mutually transcendent—mutually *co* and *ex*. At any given moment there is absolute insulation and irreducible pluralism, and yet the past experiences of each self are literally in God just as God's past experiences are literally in each present moment of human experience. Again, one can make certain distinctions between the way God experiences the past experience of other selves and the way human individuals experience the past experiences of other selves, including the divine self, but in principle they are similar.

Whitehead's account of the relation between God and a human being is the subject of some debate. His explicit position in *Process and Reality* is that God is a single concrescing actual entity and not a series of divine occasions. Most Whiteheadians, however, have adopted the Hartshornian position that God is not a single concrescing entity but rather a serially ordered society of divine occasions. There are good reasons to suppose that Whitehead himself was moving toward this position. In fact, Whitehead's concluding remarks in *Process and Reality* regarding God and the World, seem to indicate that he understands the relation between God and the World in the same manner that James does in his "Miller-Bode" notebooks. Whitehead maintains:

> It is as true to say that the World is immanent in God, as that God is immanent in the World.
> It is as true to say that God transcends the World, as that the World transcends God.
> It is as true to say that God creates the World, as that the World creates God.[19]

This process view of the relations between God and a given individual, or God and the World, which both James and Whitehead ascribe to, necessarily implies that God has an environment and that God is in some respects limited in power and knowledge. Both James and Whitehead accept this view of God, but for different reasons. Whitehead's understanding of God's limitations follows from metaphysical principles whereas James's understanding of God (at least as developed in *A Pluralistic Universe*) is merely an ad hoc solution to the problem of evil. Faced with the problem of why, if God is all powerful, all knowing, and all good, there is evil, James simply declares that God cannot be all powerful or all knowing or that God is neither all powerful nor all knowing. "The line of least resistance, then, as it seems to me, both in theology and in philosophy, is to accept, along with the superhuman consciousness, the notion that it is not all-embracing, the notion, in other words, that there *is* a God, but that he is finite, either in power or in knowledge, or both at once."[20] James's notion that God is in some respects limited, i.e., has an environment and lacks the ability to control every aspect of reality or the ability to know everything, or lacks both at once, is his solution to the problem of evil. Evil can exist because God is not in complete control or because God is partially ignorant of what is happening or because God is both ignorant and partially powerless.

For Whitehead, however, the limitation of God's power and the limitation of God's knowledge are merely the exemplification of general metaphysical principles. (Whitehead views God as the chief exemplification of all metaphysical principles.) God's power is limited because strictly contemporary actual entities do not interact and because all actual entities are, to some extent, self-determining. God influences everything that happens but God cannot strictly determine anything. As for God's knowledge, it is limited to what has already happened. There is nothing actual that God does not know but because the future is not actual, God does not and cannot know precisely what will happen. (Of course God's perfect knowledge of all that has happened allows God to know what will almost certainly happen in some cases, but the difference between "almost certain knowledge" and "absolute knowledge" is extremely important from a metaphysical standpoint.)

James could have concluded that God is in some respects limited because of the directional or asymmetrical relationship that exists between God and an individual (and between God and the World) and because experiences are partially self-determining. In point of fact, however, it is the problem of evil that prompts this position; at least in *A Pluralistic Universe* it is the problem of evil that requires James to adopt this understanding of God.

The third type of relation that James comments on is the relation between an individual and the nonhuman world, especially in terms of "knowing" and "being known." For a number of reasons James is least clear about this type of relation. When one attempts to piece together his phenomenism, his theory of universals, and his inclination for a type of representationalism, the pieces do not fit. Had James been more consistent in his process panexperiential realism, and had he realized that knowing was simply another type of relation, he could have developed a more realistic theory of knowing than he in fact did.

In his "Miller-Bode" notebooks, *The Meaning of Truth*, and *Some Problems of Philosophy*, James endorses the existence of "universals" or "eternal objects."

What I am affirming here is the platonic doctrine that concepts are singulars, that concept-stuff is inalterable, and that physical realities are constituted by various concept-stuffs of which they "partake." It is known as "logical realism" in the history of philosophy; and has been more favored by rationalistic than by empiricist minds. . . . The present book *[Some Problems of Philosophy]*, which treats concrete percepts as primordial and concepts as of secondary origin, may be regarded as somewhat eccentric in its attempt to combine logical realism with an otherwise empiricist mode of thought.[21]

In his "Miller-Bode" notebooks he writes: "Concepts . . . are eternal objects, and not psychological contents, or experiences *in concreto.*"[22] He is careful to point out that the kind of being enjoyed by concepts is inferior to the temporal kind of being enjoyed by actual experiences, but he does not doubt that they exist.[23]

In a world in which there are both concrete actualities (i.e., temporal entities) and abstract universals (i.e., eternal objects) one can talk about perception in terms of entertaining the same eternal objects that inhere in some particular object. Such a theory of knowledge, however, does not account for knowing concrete actualities, for as Whitehead says, "There can only be evidence for a world of actual entities, if the immediate actual entity [i.e., a thought or moment of experience] discloses them as essential to its own composition."[24] If experience is only the experience of universals, there is no reason to suppose that there are concrete actualities. Berkeley and Hume recognize this. James's panpsychic friend, Charles A. Strong, develops what he terms "a substitutional theory of knowledge" as an alternative to a traditional representational theory of knowledge. According to Strong's theory, immediate subjective experiences are substituted for actualities (which are themselves types of experiences) and then these immediate subjective experiences are projected upon their objective referent. This act of projection constitutes consciousness. James recognizes the advantages associated with this epistemology. He says, "I can see what an alleviation it would be to almost everything,"[25] but he hesitates to accept it. James knows that a representational epistemology, even if it is called "substitutional," is not the answer. Representationalism, or substitutionalism, does not close the gap between the knower and the known.

With his phenomenism, James has a method for explaining the immediate experience of concrete actualities: the concrete actuality and the experience of it are the same fact taken in two separate contexts. But this explanation is not realistic. A pen of pure experience that is not for anyone—that does not function as anyone's experience of it—is nothing, because it is not for itself either.

In his "Miller-Bode" notebooks James suggests an alternative to phenomenism on the one hand and representationalism or substitutionalism on the other; he suggests that knowing is an asymmetrical relation in which things that have been experiences *for themselves* are included in the experience of another.

> Turning to my own particular puzzle, how shall we translate this? The "pen," as a living real, is the name of a business centre, a "firm." It has many customers, my mind, e.g., and the physical world. To call it the *same* pen both times would mean that although my mind and the physical world can and may eventually figure in one and the same transaction, they need not do so . . . and that in respect to this particular pen-experience neither *counts* in the transaction which the other is carrying on. Neither *is counted* by the other, neither is *for* the other. All such coming and going and alternation connects with the general notion of being counted, observed, associated, or ignored and left separate. These are essentially psychic expressions so that the constitution of reality which I am making for is of [the] psychic type. . . .[26]

The pen, which is not a pen of "pure experience" but rather a "living pen"—a pen comprised of psychic events that are for themselves—may be an object in someone else's experience. The day after he made the above remark, he realized that there is no paradox in God's knowing, and thereby including, a moment of human experience, so long as one considers knowing to be a nonreciprocal or asymmetrical relation. The implication is clear: for a panexperientialist, the way in which one knows a pen is the same as the way in which God knows a particular moment of human awareness—an event, or a collection of events that were first for themselves are in a subsequent moment for another.

Whitehead's theory of perception is complex and not easy to summarize, but it is basically similar to the epistemology that James hinted at in his "Miller-Bode" notebooks. According to Whitehead, there are two "pure modes" of perception —"perception in the mode of causal efficacy" and "perception in the mode of presentational immediacy." Ordinary conscious perception is always a mixture of these two pure modes. Perception in the mode of causal efficacy is the more basic but also the vaguer mode of perception; it is the means by which a present moment of experience is aware of past moments of experience and as such is the same thing as power or physical influence. For Whitehead: "the problem of perception and the problem of power are one and the same, at least so far as perception is reduced to mere prehension of actual entities. Perception, in the sense of consciousness of such prehension, requires the additional factor of the conceptual prehension of eternal objects, and a process of integration of the two factors."[27] For Whitehead, perception in the mode of causal efficacy is the direct awareness, however vague, that past actualities are constituent in any present moment of experience. "Prehension" is his technical term for the way in which a moment of experience includes past actualities. Perception in the mode of presentational immediacy is the conceptual prehension of eternal objects and the projection of them into contemporary regions of space. In contrast to perception in the mode of causal efficacy, perception in the mode of presentational immediacy is clear and distinct, but it is also abstract. Those things present in the mode of presentational immediacy are derivatives of experiences given in the mode of causal efficacy. Using a diagram similar to the ones used to illustrate the relation between one person and another and between God and a particular person, one can depict Whitehead's theory of perception in the following manner:

A   〉   〉   〉   〉   〉

e   〉   〉   〉   〉   〉

f   〉   〉   〉   〉   〉

Time   1   2   3   4   5

If the series of events labeled A represents a human person, and if the series of events labeled e and f represent enduring objects, then past events e_{1-4}, A_{1-4}, and f_{1-4} are perceived in A_5 through the mode of causal efficacy and the regions of space occupied by the occasions e_5 and f_5 are objectified by A_5 through the mode of presentational immediacy. The actual occasions e_5 and f_5 are not themselves directly perceived by A_5, rather, data derived from antecedent occasions that are directly perceived are projected into those regions of space that e_5 and f_5 occupy.

Admittedly this is an oversimplified account of Whitehead's theory of perception. For Whitehead the perception of a pen, for example, involves more than the integration of one series of actualities perceived in the mode of causal efficacy and the projection of eternal objects or universals into a contemporary region of space. A pen is not simply *a* series of actualities; a pen is comprised of a countless number of series of electronic, atomic, and molecular events. What is perceived are vast societies of very similar events. The above model, however, is schematically correct. It conveys the points that strictly contemporary actualities are not directly perceived, that past actualities are literally constitutive of present actualities, and that "the problem of perception," at least insofar as perception is limited to the prehension of actual entities, is the same as the "problem of power" (or "the problem of causal relatedness"). At least schematically, the way in which God is affected by the world—the way in which the world works upon God—for example, can be diagrammed in the same manner as the way a pen affects or works upon a human individual. For Whitehead, internal relations are prehensions.[28]

As a consistent process panexperientialist for whom everything actual is first an experience for itself and subsequently an experience for others, Whitehead is able to develop a general theory of relations. Past actualities are internally related to present actualities; contemporary actualities are externally related. Like James, Whitehead believes that things are in some ways together and in some other ways separate and that these ways are distinguishable. And also like James, Whitehead believes that to affect something is to get inside of it somehow, that relations are given in experience, and that knowing is essentially a nonreciprocal or asymmetrical relation. Unlike James, however, Whitehead constructs a general theory of relations.

What is the Status of Formal Logic vis-à-vis Reality?   Closely related to the topic of relations is the topic of logic. In *A Pluralistic Universe* James believes it necessary to give up logic in order to account for causal relations. Whitehead, on the other hand, was instrumental in constructing what is now known as the logic of relations. It is important to point out that the logic James gives up "fairly, squarely, and irrevocably" is not the type of logic Whitehead subscribes to and helped formulate.

James rejects what he calls "intellectualistic logic" or what is generally known as the "logic of identity" or "subject/predicate logic." According to the logic of identity, there are subjects with attributes. Subjects are defined in terms of their attributes and cannot change, for if a subject were to undergo change, it would assume new attributes and thus would not be the same subject. Speaking of the logic of identity, James remarks: "The classic extreme in this direction is the denial of the possibility of change, and the consequent branding of the world of change as unreal, by certain philosophers. The definition of A is changeless, so is the definition of B. The one definition cannot change into the other, so the notion that a concrete thing A should change into another concrete thing B is made out to be contrary to reason."[29] The logic of identity presupposes that concrete actualities can be defined solely in terms of changeless universals. Consequently, concrete actualities are themselves considered to be changeless. A thing is forever just what it is. Moreover, because concrete things can be defined solely in terms of universals, the relation between one concrete thing and another is not essential to either actuality. Relations are purely accidental.

Unwilling to accept a world in which things are changeless and where concrete things are not defined in terms of their relations to other concrete things, James rejects the logic of identity. "I myself find no good warrant for even suspecting the existence of any reality of a higher denomination than that distributed and strung-along and flowing sort of reality which we finite beings swim in. That is the sort of reality given us, and that is the sort with which logic [the logic of identity] is so incommensurable."[30]

About the same time that James was rejecting the logic of identity "fairly, squarely, and irrevocably," Frege, Whitehead, and Russell were revolutionizing logic with the introduction of the "logic of relatives" or what is now termed the "logic of relations." The logic of relations assumes that the relation of subject to predicate, or a member of a class to a class, or of a class to another class, is far from being the only fundamental relations into which subjects enter. "Rather the relation of a subject to other subjects, Rabc . . . is the essential or general principle, of which 'S is P' is the special case in which the other subjects S', S'' . . . are vacuous."[31] The logic of relations, which includes the logic of identity, affirms what the logic of identity denies, i.e., that a subject may enter into and affect another subject. Because certain kinds of relations are internal to one term and external to the other, subjects may include other subjects. The relations of knowing, loving, or hating include what is known, loved, or hated—knowing x, loving y, hating z. The effect includes the cause, or, more generally stated, the feeling-of-x must include x, otherwise it is merely the feeling-of-.

James knew of the existence of the logic of relations, but to what extent he understood it is not known. In all probability he was not sufficiently versed in it to make a judgment on it one way or another. Less than a year before his death in 1910 he writes in a letter to Arthur O. Lovejoy: "If continuity and flow mean logical self-contradiction, then logic must go. B. Russell's disciples pretend that he has saved logic by the 'new' infinite. Perhaps he has, and if so the better, but I wait to be convinced."[32] As far as I know, James was never convinced. But what is important to note is that the type of logic he rejects is not the type of logic that Whitehead affirms, and James's reasons for rejecting the logic of identity do not apply to the logic of relations. In fact, to the extent that James endorses the notion that instances of actuality enjoy various types of relations—e.g., asymmetrical relations in which one term is internal to the other while the other term is external to it, and asymmetrical relations where both terms are external to each other—he could have supported this logic of relations.

In this final chapter my intent has been to show how James might have developed his central insights and his most salient concepts into a coherent system. In my estimation Whitehead's process philosophy provides the basis for just such a development. This is hardly coincidental; one of Whitehead's aims was to "rescue" James's philosophy, along with Bergson's and Dewey's philosophies, from the charges of anti-intellectualism. I think that Whitehead succeeds in this.

Postscript

This book does not capture the spirit of William James; it does not capture his wit, his charm, his thoughtfulness, his hypochondria, and everything else that made him the lovable genius that he was. I felt no need to perform this formidable task because it has been done so well by Perry and, less well, by others. Still, I regret having dealt with James so coldly.

Apart from its absence of warmth, I suspect that there will be those who criticize this book for explaining away some of James's thought while others will object, not because I have explained away some of James, but because I have explained away the wrong stuff. I *meant* to explain away some of James. I do not believe that everything he said is of equal significance. Moreover, I think that James was continuously revising some of his ideas, and that his philosophy did not emerge full-grown but rather developed over time. He intended some of his later concepts to reverse some of his earlier ones.

Whether or not I have explained away the right stuff is a more complicated matter. I have taken into consideration how often James endorsed a particular position and how emphatically. For instance, James was most emphatic on the matter of being a metaphysical realist. Those notions that crop up over and over again and those that James emphasized I have taken to be more "Jamesian." Also, I have considered the context in which a statement was made, or a position developed, and the date. Generally, I have placed more stress on those positions that he held toward the end of his life than on those held relatively early. My decisions about what to keep of James and what to explain away may be mistaken, but they were not arbitrary.

In the introduction I mentioned that I think that James was right—that reality is in fact the way he believed it to be, or nearly so. This is a dangerous confession because it calls into question my objectivity. If I have misconstrued James's philosophy, I did not mean to. If there is another way of holding together his insights and his beliefs that is more inclusive, more consistent, and more illuminating, I will adopt that new perspective. Still, it seems to me that there is a plurality of actualities, that the sum total of actualities is increasing, that the self is actually a series of experiences, that relations are felt, that to exist is to be or to have been an experience for oneself, that to act on anything means to get into it somehow, that some relations (including knowing) are asymmetrical, and that God is active but is also limited in some respects. And it seems to me that these beliefs and insights are central to James's philosophy.

List of Abbreviations

Except where noted, all works are by William James.

CER   *Collected Essays and Reviews*. Edited with preface and notes by Ralph Barton Perry. New York: Longmans, Green and Co., 1920.

ERE   *Essays in Radical Empiricism*. 1912. Reprint. Cambridge: Harvard University Press, 1976. Textual editor Fredson Bowers, associate editor Ignas K. Skrupskelis. Introduction by John J. McDermott.

Imm   *Human Immortality: Two Supposed Objections to the Doctrine*. Boston: Houghton Mifflin, 1898. Second ed. with preface containing replies to criticisms, 1899.

MS   *Memories and Studies*. Edited with prefatory note by Henry James, Jr. New York: Longmans, Green and Co., 1911.

MT   *The Meaning of Truth, A Sequel to Pragmatism*. 1909. Cambridge: Harvard University Press, 1975. Reprint. Textual editor Fredson Bowers, associate editor Ignas K. Skrupskelis. Introduction by H. S. Thayer.

PP   *The Principles of Psychology*. 2 vols. New York: Henry Holt and Co., 1890.

Prag   *Pragmatism: A New Name for Some Old Ways of Thinking*. 1907. Cambridge: Harvard University Press, 1975. Reprint. Textual editor Fredson Bowers, associate editor Ignas K. Skrupskelis. Introduction by H. S. Thayer.

Psy   *Psychology: Briefer Course*. New York: Henry Holt and Co., 1892.

PU   *A Pluralistic Universe*. Hibbert Lectures at Manchester College on the Present Situation in Philosophy. 1909. Cambridge: Harvard University Press, 1977. Reprint. Textual editor Fredson Bowers, associate editor Ignas K. Skrupskelis. Introduction by Richard J. Bernstein.

SPP   *Some Problems of Philosophy. A Beginning of an Introduction to Philosophy*. Edited with prefatory note by Henry James, Jr. Prepared for the press by H. M. Kallen. New York: Longmans, Green and Co., 1911.

TCWJ   Ralph Barton Perry. *The Thought and Character of William James*. 2 vols. Boston: Little, Brown and Co., 1935.

VRE   *The Varieties of Religious Experience: A Study in Human Nature*. New York: Longmans, Green and Co., 1902.

WB   *The Will to Believe, and Other Essays in Popular Philosophy*. 1894. Reprint. Cambridge: Harvard University Press, 1979. Edited by Frederick H. Burkhardt, Fredson Bowers, and Ignas K. Skrupskelis. Introduction by Edward H. Madden.

Notes

Introduction

1. See Bruce Kuklick, *The Rise of American Philosophy* (New Haven: Yale University Press, 1977), pp. 323–26, 331–34. Wendel T. Bush also recognized James's attraction to panpsychism. In his 1925 article, "William James and Panpsychism," Bush concluded, "James' pronouncements on panpsychism are scattered, tentative and metaphorical—but full of personal confidence. It is a pity from the point of view of literature, that he never gave complete and systematic expression of his views, for it would have been so imaginative and so human a document." See *Studies in the History of Ideas,* ed. Department of Philosophy of Columbia University (New York: Columbia University Press, 1925), 2:326.
2. See Edward H. Madden and Peter Hare, "The Powers that Be," *Dialogue* 10 (1971):12–31. See also Madden and Hare, "A Critical Appraisal of James's View of Causality," in *The Philosophy of William James,* ed. Walter Robert Corti (Hamburg: Felix Meiner Verlag, 1976).
3. Bruce Wilshire, "Protophenomenology in the Psychology of William James," *Transactions of the Charles S. Peirce Society* 5 (Winter 1969): 41.
4. Henry Levinson, *Science, Metaphysics and the Chance of Salvation: An Interpretation of the Thought of William James* (Missoula, Mont.: Scholars Press, 1978), p. 111.
5. Psy., pp. 461–62.
6. Ibid., p. 461.
7. TCWJ, 2:604.
8. CER, pp. 443–44.
9. See TCWJ, 2:764.
10. Ibid., p. 287.
11. WB, p. 77.
12. See TCWJ, 2:583.
13. CER, p. 451.
14. SPP, p. viii.

Chapter 1

1. James also discusses the "conscious automaton-theory." I will not present his arguments against this theory because his opposition to it is so well known. "On *a priori* and quasi-metaphysical grounds," he says, "[it] is an *unwarrantable impertinence in the present state of psychology*" and "... the circumstantial evidence against that theory is strong" (PP, 1:138, 144).

2. PP, 1:145, 146.

3. Ibid., p. 149. Technically, the "mind-dust theory" may be held in one of two forms: each aboriginal atom of consciousness may be linked to a particular atom of the physical universe; or each aboriginal atom of consciousness may exist independently of the physical atoms of the universe and yet, susceptible to being focused or compounded by the physical atoms of the animal brain.

4. See PP, 1:344, 161.

5. Ibid., p. 160.

6. James briefly considers the "material-monad theory" as a means of circumventing the problems that beset the mind-stuff theory but dismisses it on the basis that such a position is no more empirically verifiable than the mind-stuff theory. No one has ever observed a monad. In his estimation, "Leibnitzian monadism" is a self-consistent doctrine but it is so remote and unreal as to be almost useless to the psychologist. See PP, 1:179–80.

7. Ibid., p. 277.

8. Quoted by James in PP, 1:351, from David Hume's *A Treatise on Human Understanding*, bk. 1, pt. 4, sec. 6.

9. Quoted by James in PP, 1:352, from David Hume's *A Treatise on Human Understanding*, Appendix to bk. 1.

10. David Hume, *A Treatise on Human Nature*, bk. 1, pt. 4, sec. 5.

11. PP, 1:354.

12. Ibid., 1:343–44, 365.

13. Ibid., 1:344.

14. Ibid., 1:348, 365, 369–70.

15. Ibid., p. 342.

16. Ibid., p. 400, his emphasis.

17. Ibid., p. 225, his emphasis.

18. Ibid., pp. 226, 227–29.

19. Ibid., p. 234.

20. Ibid., pp. 245–46.

21. Ibid., p. 331.

22. Ibid., p. 340.

23. VRE, pp. 233–34.

24. PP, 1:163.

25. Psy., p. 468.

26. William James, *Principii di psicologia* (Milan: Società editrice libraria, 1909), p. ix.

27. Psy., pp. 466–67.

28. PP, 1:239.

29. Psy., p. 467.

30. Charles Hartshorne, *Creative Synthesis and Philosophic Method* (La Salle: Open Court Publishing Co., 1970), pp. 194–95.

31. PP, 1:148–50.

Chapter 2

1. I am indebted to Edward H. Madden for pointing out this grouping of the ten essays. See Madden's introduction to the Harvard University Press edition of *The Will to Believe, and Other Essays in Popular Philosophy.*
2. William James, *Essays in Philosophy*, intro. John J. McDermott (Cambridge: Harvard University Press, 1978), p. 116.
3. See TCWJ, 1:490–91.
4. Ibid., p. 478.
5. See PP, 1:138–42. See also James's essay "Are We Automata?,"*Mind* 4 (1879).
6. See TCWJ, 1:323.
7. Ibid., p. 682.
8. PP, 1:149, his emphasis.
9. At the time James wrote this he did not believe in nonconscious experiences. Later, of course, he accepts the position that not all experiences are conscious experiences. His statement that evolution cannot work smoothly if consciousness in some form is not present in the very beginning, would, in light of his later view, have to be amended to read: if evolution is to work smoothly, experience in some form must have been there at the very beginning. Conscious experiences could evolve from nonconscious experiences but experience as such could not evolve from nonexperiencing things.
10. WB, pp. 111–12.
11. Ibid., p. 164.
12. Ibid., p. 167, his emphasis.
13. Ibid., p. 135.
14. Ibid., p. 129, his emphasis.
15. Ibid., pp. 138–40.
16. Ibid., p. 103.
17. Ibid., pp. 52, 32.
18. Ibid., p. 33.
19. Ibid., pp. 28, 26, 56.
20. Ibid., p. 55.
21. Ibid., p. 161.
22. Ibid., pp. 241, 239.
23. Ibid., p. 236.

Chapter 3

1. See TCWJ, 1:817.
2. Imm., p. 27.
3. Ibid., my emphasis.
4. Ibid., his emphasis.
5. VRE, p. 515, his emphasis. Note that James specifically says "continuous."
6. Ibid., pp. 515–16.
7. Ibid., pp. 521, 516–17 n.2.
8. See TCWJ, 2:583, his emphasis.
9. PU, pp. 130, 132.
10. Ibid., pp. 54–55, 26.
11. Ibid., pp. 19–20, 16, 19.
12. Ibid., p. 55, his emphasis.

13. Ibid., p. 147.
14. Prag., pp. 139–40.
15. PU, pp. 55–56.
16. Ibid., p. 33.
17. Ibid., p. 41.
18. Ibid., p. 33, my emphasis.
19. Ibid., pp. 113, 121.
20. Ibid., p. 57.
21. Ibid., p. 60, his emphasis.
22. Ibid., p. 132, my emphasis.
23. Ibid., pp. 130, 129–30.
24. Ibid., p. 139, my emphasis.
25. Ibid., p. 145, my emphasis. In his "Miller-Bode" notebooks (1905–1908) James writes: " 'I' can be, and be known; be, and have another being next to me; why can't I have another being own and use me, just as I am for its purposes, without knowing those purposes myself" (See TCWJ, 2:765). Note how James associates being included with being "owned" and "used."
26. Ibid., p. 140. See also p. 61.
27. The fact that James suggests that God is limited "either in power or knowledge, or in both" probably indicates that he did not realize his assumption that to include is to control, for if inclusion or knowledge entails power, there would be no need to say "or in both."
28. Ibid., p. 41.
29. TCWJ, 2:598.
30. MS, p. 204, my emphasis.

Chapter 4

1. Ayer uses this term in his introduction to the 1978 Harvard Paperback edition of William James's *Pragmatism*, p. xxx.
2. WB, p. 26.
3. MT, p. 8.
4. F. C. S. Schiller, *Humanism* (London: Macmillan and Co., Ltd., 1903), p. xvii.
5. Ibid., p. xx.
6. In his later writings Schiller reluctantly accepts the distinction between "finding" and "making" the real, but at the same time he restates the meaninglessness of the "real-as-it-is-in-itself."
7. MT, p. 46.
8. Prag., p. 122.
9. Notice that in the above quotation James says that "altho the stubborn fact remains that there is a sensible flux, what is *true of it* [his emphasis] seems from first to last to be *largely* [my emphasis] a matter of our own creation." It is, I think, important to emphasize that he says "largely" rather than "completely" or "totally," which is what Schiller would have said.
10. CER, p. 451.
11. MT, p. 132.
12. See TCWJ, 2:509.
13. F. C. S. Schiller, *Humanism*, p. 11 n.1.
14. In fairness to both men, one must conclude that there are *at least* two

types of pragmatism, one that is realistic and one that is not. In his book, *Present Philosophical Tendencies* (New York: Longmans, Green and Co., 1912), Ralph Barton Perry makes just such a distinction. "Some pragmatists, such as James, are avowedly, and on the whole consistently, realistic. Others, such as Schiller, favor, if they do not unequivocally adopt, the subjective alternative. . . . A realistic pragmatist will in his epistemology describe the sensible facts of nature as the termini to which ideas lead, but *he will not suppose that such facts must be thus related to ideas in order to be*. Sensible facts are occasionally and accidentally the termini of ideas, but not essentially so" (p. 214, my emphasis). In his article "May a Realist be a Pragmatist," *Journal of Philosophy* 6 (1909), W. P. Montague differentiates four types of pragmatism: biological or instrumental pragmatism, psychological pragmatism, ontological pragmatism or humanism, and logical pragmatism. In Montague's estimation "a realist might be a pragmatist of the biological or instrumentalist type, and . . . an instrumentalist, to make his theory consistent, would have to adopt a realistic standpoint." Arthur O. Lovejoy differentiates thirteen types of pragmatisms.

15. MT, p. 128.
16. Ibid., p. 158.
17. To say that truths are not subject to change does not mean that that which will be true in the future is already true now. New actualities bring about new propositions, some of which are true, others false. Propositions concerning already existing actualities, however, are already true or false and are not subject to change.
18. MT, p. 155.
19. Prag., p. 97, his emphasis.
20. Ibid., p. 98.
21. MT, p. 63.
22. Prag., pp. 106–7, 98, 100.
23. MT, pp. 110, 155, 95–96.
24. Ibid., p. 110.
25. Ibid., p. 56, his emphasis.
26. See H. S. Thayer's introduction to the 1975 Harvard University Press edition of *The Meaning of Truth*. See also Thayer's article, "On William James on Truth," *Transactions of the Charles S. Peirce Society* 12 (1977): 3–19.
27. See H. S. Thayer's introduction to the 1975 Harvard University Press edition of *The Meaning of Truth*, pp. xlii–xliii.
28. Thayer has subsequently argued that propositions about future actualities are already true or false. See "James and the Theory of Truth," *Transactions of the Charles S. Peirce Society* 16 (1980): 39–48.
29. See TCWJ, 2:476–77, his emphasis.
30. See TCWJ, 2:478.
31. WB, pp. 27–33.
32. MT, p. 57.
33. See TCWJ, 2:485.
34. MT, p. 305. See also pp. 151–53.
35. Ibid., p. 156.
36. SPP, p. 106. See also MT, p. 52 n.4.
37. See TCWJ, 2:758, his emphasis.
38. Ibid., 2:477, 550.

Chapter 5

1. PP, pp. 148–49, his emphasis.
2. See TCWJ, 2:373.
3. VRE, p. 499, his emphasis.
4. Ibid., p. 501 n.1.
5. CER, pp. 443–44.
6. See TCWJ, 2:550.
7. ERE, pp. 4, 39. See also p. 110, "La Notion de Conscience."
8. Ibid., p. 61. At one point James qualifies this first meaning of "pure experience" saying: "Although for fluency's sake I myself spoke early in this article of a stuff of pure experience, I have now to say that there is no *general* stuff of which experience at large is made. There are as many stuffs as there are 'natures' in things experienced" (ERE, pp. 14–15). At first glance this appears to constitute still another meaning of "pure experience." It does not function, however, as a new meaning in James's philosophy. James's statement that there are "as many stuffs as there are 'natures' in things experienced" functions only to emphasize that pure experiences are neutral in terms of ontological or qualitative dualisms.
9. Ibid., p. 8.
10. See TCWJ, 2:550.
11. Ibid., p. 46. James continues: "If now we ask why we must thus translate experience from a more concrete or pure form into a more intellectualized form, filling it with ever more abounding conceptual form . . . [the] naturalist answer is that the environment kills as well as sustains us, and that the tendency of raw experience to extinguish the experient himself is lessened just in the degree in which the elements in it that have a practical bearing upon life are analyzed out of the continuum and verbally fixed and coupled together so that we may know what is in the wind for us and get ready to react next time." Note the similarity of this passage to Hartshorne's explanation as to why individual thoughts or moments of experience are not consciously experienced. See chapter 2.
12. Ibid., p. 47.
13. Ibid., pp. 43, 66.
14. Ibid., pp. 43, 95.
15. B. H. Bode, " 'Pure Experience' and the External World," *Journal of Philosophy* 2 (1905): 133.
16. B. H. Bode, "The Concept of Pure Experience," *Philosophical Review* 14 (1905): 695.
17. See TCWJ, 2:446.
18. Ibid., p. 764, his emphasis.
19. PU, pp. 141–42.
20. SPP, p. 218. James makes a similar allusion in Prag., p. 138.
21. MS, p. 204.
22. Bruce Kuklick is an exception, and he shares my assessment that James finally endorses panpsychism. In *The Rise of American Philosophy*, Kuklick writes: "Analyzing experience brought him . . . to panpsychism and a view that knowing constituted existence. This position extricated him from the problems of possible experience and the mutuality of experience. James did not need the possible because the actual was mutable: each pulse of experience could, at the same time, be what it was for itself and what it was for us" (pp. 333–34).

My only disagreement with Kuklick's position is that he views pan-psychism as a form of ontological or metaphysical idealism rather than as a form of ontological or metaphysical realism. His reasoning is quite clear. If metaphysical realism is the position that objects exist independently of *all* experience—he says independently of all "consciousness"—and if panpsychism is the position that everything actual is self-experiencing, i.e., is for itself, then panpsychism is not a form of metaphysical realism because it does not allow for the existence of "objects" independently of their own experience. Kuklick's conclusion is correct if one accepts his definition of "metaphysical realism" but I think his definition misses the focus of the realist/idealist debate. The major issue between the metaphysical realist and the metaphysical idealist is *not* whether objects may exist independently of *all* experience but rather whether objects may exist independently of anyone else's experience of them. The idealists say "No," the realists say "Yes." If this is in fact the heart of the realist/idealist debate then panpsychism is a species of metaphysical or ontological realism because it contends that things may exist independently of anyone's else's experience of them.

23. ERE, p. 39, my emphasis.

24. It should be noted that, as he did in his psychology, James continued to vacillate between thinking of processes as continuous "streams" and thinking of them as series or "chains" of events. On June 13, 1907, he wrote to Henri Bergson concerning the latter's recently published *L'Evolution créatrice*. "I feel that at bottom we are fighting the same fight. . . . The position we are rescuing is 'Tychism' and a really growing world. But where as I have hitherto found no better way of defending Tychism than by affirming the spontaneous addition of *discrete* elements of being . . . , thereby playing the same game with intellectualist weapons, you set things straight at a single stroke by your fundamental conception of the continuously creative nature of reality" (See TCWJ, 2:619).

James considers Bergson's major contribution to be the idea that change is continuous or streamlike rather than discontinuous or chainlike. Although he believes that Bergson "set things straight" he did not understand how a continuum could act. Without real individuals, i.e., discrete moments of experience which are at least partially self-determining, how is action possible? James continues: "With a frank pluralism of *beings* endowed with vital impulses you can get oppositions and compromises easily enough, and a stagnant deposit; but after my one reading [of *L'Evolution créatrice*] I don't exactly 'catch on' to the way in which the continuum of reality resists itself so as to have to act, etc., etc." (See TCWJ, 2:620). There can be no action apart from *individuals* who possess some agency.

25. See TCWJ, 2:764.

26. PU, pp. 113, 117.

27. TCWJ, 2:764–65, his emphasis.

28. Ibid., p. 765, his emphasis.

Chapter 6

1. Craig Eisendrath, *The Unifying Moment: The Psychological Philosophy of William James and Alfred North Whitehead* (Cambridge: Harvard University Press, 1971), p. xiii.

2. I believe that Eisendrath's book is primarily a book about James's thought and not about Whitehead's thought or the relation between James's philosophy and Whitehead's. Furthermore, I have a good many disagreements with Eisendrath's position as I understand it. But I do agree with his basic thesis that certain aspects of James's and Whitehead's philosophies are extremely compatible and that reading one can lead to a better understanding of the other.

3. Alfred North Whitehead, *Process and Reality: Corrected Edition,* ed. David R. Griffin and Donald W. Sherburne (1929; New York: The Free Press, 1978), p. 18.

4. SPP, p. 218.

5. ERE, p. 43.

6. See TCWJ, 2:446.

7. PP, 1:339.

8. See TCWJ, 2:764.

9. PU, pp. 40–41.

10. MT, p. 7.

11. PP, pp. 225–26.

12. ERE, p. 25, my emphasis.

13. PU, p. 100.

14. Whitehead, *Process and Reality,* p. 20.

15. Ibid., p. 32.

16. VRE, p. 517 n.2.

17. PU, p. 132.

18. See TCWJ, 2:765.

19. Whitehead, *Process and Reality,* p. 348.

20. PU, p. 141.

21. SPP, p. 106.

22. See TCWJ, 2:751.

23. Because he regarded logical or Platonic realism as the first step toward rationalism or "conceptualism," James's endorsement of universals had a strong nominalistic bent. This is apparent in the above quotations from *Some Problems of Philosophy* where he spoke of concepts as having a "secondary origin." James was dead set against the rationalistic tendency to prefer universals to the concrete actualities, and it is because of this that he qualified his Platonic realism. According to James, "Rationalistic thought, with its exclusive interest in the unchanging and the general, has always de-realized the passing pulses of life. . . . The belief in the genuineness of each particular moment in which we feel the squeeze of this world's life, as we actually do work here, or work is done upon us, is the Eden from which rationalists seek in vain to expel us" (SPP, p. 110). The fact that James spoke of universals as "eternal objects," however, indicates that by "secondary origin" he did not mean that they were derived from perception, but rather that they are less actual than concrete actualities. Eternal objects cannot meaningfully be said to be derived from temporal experiences.

24. Whitehead, *Process and Reality,* p. 145.

25. See TCWJ, 2:536.

26. Ibid., p. 764.

27. Whitehead, *Process and Reality,* p. 58.

28. See Victor Lowe's excellent article "William James and Whitehead's Doctrine of Prehension," *Journal of Philosophy* 38 (Fall 1941): 113–

25, for an interesting and more detailed exploration of James and Whitehead on the matter of prehensions and internal relations.

29. PU, p. 100.
30. Ibid., p. 97.
31. Charles Hartshorne, *Creative Synthesis and Philosophic Method*, p. 82.
32. See TCWJ, 2:596–97.

Index